WEST-E

Family and Consumer Sciences Education (041)

SECRETS

Study Guide
Your Key to Exam Success

WEST-E Test Review for the
Washington Educator Skills Tests - Endorsements

Dear Future Exam Success Story:

Congratulations on your purchase of our study guide. Our goal in writing our study guide was to cover the content on the test, as well as provide insight into typical test taking mistakes and how to overcome them.

Standardized tests are a key component of being successful, which only increases the importance of doing well in the high-pressure high-stakes environment of test day. How well you do on this test will have a significant impact on your future, and we have the research and practical advice to help you execute on test day.

The product you're reading now is designed to exploit weaknesses in the test itself, and help you avoid the most common errors test takers frequently make.

How to use this study guide

We don't want to waste your time. Our study guide is fast-paced and fluff-free. We suggest going through it a number of times, as repetition is an important part of learning new information and concepts.

First, read through the study guide completely to get a feel for the content and organization. Read the general success strategies first, and then proceed to the content sections. Each tip has been carefully selected for its effectiveness.

Second, read through the study guide again, and take notes in the margins and highlight those sections where you may have a particular weakness.

Finally, bring the manual with you on test day and study it before the exam begins.

Your success is our success

We would be delighted to hear about your success. Send us an email and tell us your story. Thanks for your business and we wish you continued success.

Sincerely,

Mometrix Test Preparation Team

Need more help? Check out our flashcards at: http://MometrixFlashcards.com/WEST

TABLE OF CONTENTS

Top 20 Test Taking Tips

1. Carefully follow all the test registration procedures
2. Know the test directions, duration, topics, question types, how many questions
3. Setup a flexible study schedule at least 3-4 weeks before test day
4. Study during the time of day you are most alert, relaxed, and stress free
5. Maximize your learning style; visual learner use visual study aids, auditory learner use auditory study aids
6. Focus on your weakest knowledge base
7. Find a study partner to review with and help clarify questions
8. Practice, practice, practice
9. Get a good night's sleep; don't try to cram the night before the test
10. Eat a well balanced meal
11. Know the exact physical location of the testing site; drive the route to the site prior to test day
12. Bring a set of ear plugs; the testing center could be noisy
13. Wear comfortable, loose fitting, layered clothing to the testing center; prepare for it to be either cold or hot during the test
14. Bring at least 2 current forms of ID to the testing center
15. Arrive to the test early; be prepared to wait and be patient
16. Eliminate the obviously wrong answer choices, then guess the first remaining choice
17. Pace yourself; don't rush, but keep working and move on if you get stuck
18. Maintain a positive attitude even if the test is going poorly
19. Keep your first answer unless you are positive it is wrong
20. Check your work, don't make a careless mistake

Interpersonal and Family Relationships

Direct and indirect communication

Direct communication occurs when a person who is attempting to convey a given piece of information simply states that information to the person he or she wants to receive the information. Indirect communication, on the other hand, is when the person communicating the information states the information, but not to anyone in particular. For example, if a parent says, "Christine, we need to set the table," that is an example of direct communication because the parent is addressing the person he or she wants to talk to directly. However, if the parent instead simply mutters out loud, "We need to set the table," rather than saying it to someone in particular, that would be an example of indirect communication. Direct communication is far more effective in carrying out the day-to-day functions necessary to maintain a family than indirect communication because various tasks can be assigned directly to a particular individual.

Families with individuals who use direct, clear communication are the most effective. These family members listen to one another, spend more time communicating, respect one another's points of view, and pay attention to the more subtle forms of affective communication. By communicating directly and concisely with other family members, each family member creates a much more effective form of communication than that which would be found in any other setting. If the individuals receiving the information listen to and respect their fellow family members and—more importantly—make the time to listen to them in the first place, the communication between family members will become much stronger. Of course, this communication can be strengthened even further if members of the family are careful to take note of emotional indicators that allow them to identify the feelings of another family member without that person having to verbally express his or her feelings.

Solving any given problem

A well-functioning family would first identify the problem itself and determine the cause of the problem. The family would then develop a list of solutions that could potentially solve the problem, and they would attempt to determine the benefits of each solution. After determining the benefits of each solution, the family would choose the solution that seems to best solve the problem and then, after putting the solution into effect, monitor the solution to make sure that it actually solved the problem. Finally, the family would decide whether the solution worked or not to determine whether it was necessary to try something else. This entire process is important to the functioning of a family because it prevents problems from being misdiagnosed early on and prevents them from getting too far out of control.

Social interaction

Outside social interaction is extremely important for all family members, regardless of age, because it offers an opportunity for each individual to improve his or her social skills, learn about the world around them, and learn more about values that one might not learn from the family alone. This is especially true in the case of children. Research shows that children who have regular outside social interaction, through things such as extracurricular activities, are less likely to rebel or cause problems and more likely to excel in school and relationships. Outside social interaction is also necessary for the children of a family to eventually leave the household and create families of their own, as they need to seek out their own relationships. Therefore, social interaction with individuals outside of the family is necessary not only for the fulfillment of the members of the family, but also to continue the life cycle of the family.

Conflict within a relationship

The many sources of conflict within a relationship are too numerous to mention, but some of the common problems include the following: setting expectations that are too high, not appreciating or respecting the other person in the relationship, not considering the feelings of the other person, being afraid of showing affection or emotion, being overdependent, being inflexible, expecting the other member of the relationship to change, and lacking effective communication. Preventing conflict can be extremely difficult. Preventing it altogether is virtually impossible, but avoiding some or all of these common sources of conflict can greatly reduce the number of conflicts that take place within any given relationship.

A family can successfully resolve a conflict by following steps very similar to those of the basic problem-solving model. First, the family needs to attempt to identify the problem, making sure to maintain open communication while remaining objective and minimizing hostility. After the problem is identified, the family must strive to recognize the various positions that each member has regarding the conflict while again attempting to minimize hostility. After each person involved in the conflict has made his or her position clear, the family must move toward a compromise that will work for everyone. Each step of the conflict resolution process requires that the people involved in the conflict remain as patient and as understanding as possible, which can often be extremely difficult when a solution or compromise cannot be determined immediately.

Divorce

Divorce is the termination of the union created by marriage before the death of either member of the union. It has a significant impact on the stability of the family unit as a whole, and it affects the relationships and well-being of the individual members of the family. Frequently, when the marital couple decides to divorce, there has already been significant stress placed on the entire family from the difficulties the marital couple has been experiencing. However, divorce can often lead to a great deal more stress being placed on the family, especially when children are involved. As a result, individuals within and outside the marital couple may become more withdrawn or hostile as the structure of the family changes. Divorce also allows both members of the marital couple to later remarry, as their legal obligation to each other no longer exists. This can further alter the family structure by adding stepparents to the mix.

Studies indicate that the age at which a couple marries may have a significant impact on whether they remain married for an extended period. Individuals who marry before either member of the couple is 18 will often separate within a few years of their marriage. Individuals who are in the 18–25 range will separate less frequently than those who marry before 18, but they are still at a very high risk for their marriage ending in divorce rather than death. Individuals who marry after both members of the couple are over 25 have a significantly lower risk of divorce than those who marry at younger ages. Ultimately, statistics show that the risk of divorce decreases as the age of each member of the couple at the time of the marriage increases.

There are many factors that may influence the risk of a marriage ending in divorce, including income, education, religion, pregnancy before marriage, and whether the parents of the married couple are divorced. Couples who make over $50,000 a year are at a much lower risk of divorce than couples who make less than that amount. Couples comprised of well-educated individuals who have graduated from high school and have at least some college background also have a much lower risk of divorce than less educated individuals. Couples with no religious background or drastically different religious backgrounds have a much higher risk of divorce than couples who have religious backgrounds that do not conflict. Couples who have a baby prior to being married also have a higher risk of divorce than couples who have children after they are married. Individuals with parents who are divorced also have a higher risk of divorce than individuals from intact families.

Social and economic factors

Social and economic factors affect the overall functioning of a family. In fact, researchers use an index called the socioeconomic status, or SES, to measure the ability of the family to function in a healthy fashion. The SES uses the educational background of the members of the family, the family's total income, and the skill—both actual and perceived—required by the occupations of the individuals who act as providers for the family to measure the family's ability to function. Individuals who are well-educated tend to marry later in life, receive jobs with higher incomes, and have careers with a higher social status, which all add stability to the marriage and stability to the overall functioning of the family. Families that earn a higher income are also less concerned with obtaining basic necessities because the family consistently has the means to obtain them. As a result, there is often less stress experienced by the family.

Affective communication and instrumental communication

The two primary types of communication used by family members are affective communication and instrumental communication. Affective communication is communication in which an individual demonstrates his or her feelings through facial expressions, motions, gestures, or by stating his or her feelings outright. Instrumental communication is when an individual informs another member of the family of a piece of factual information that is necessary to carry out the normal day-to-day functions of the family. An example of instrumental communication is a mother informing her child where he or she can find his or her socks. Families that use both types of communication usually function more effectively than families that use instrumental communication more often than affective communication.

Clear and masked communication

Clear communication occurs when an individual explicitly states the information he or she is trying to convey, and there is no ambiguity as to the meaning of the statement. For example, "I am upset because Daniel is not home from the movies yet" is an example of clear communication because there is no question that the individual making the statement is

- 4 -

upset at Daniel for not being home. On the other hand, masked communication occurs when an individual states the information he or she is trying to convey in a vague and somewhat confusing manner. For example, "I am upset" is an example of masked communication because there is no indication as to why the person is upset. As these examples illustrate, clear communication is always more effective in conveying a particular piece of information than masked communication.

Development and education of family members

One of the most important functions a family provides is developing and educating family members. Parents and grandparents pass their heritage and teachings of social norms and acceptable behavior to the children of the family through their customs, traditions, and ultimately their actions. Children learn about their heritage through the traditions of the family and also often learn lessons about the manner in which they are expected to behave by using the behavior of their parents and the rest of the household as a model for how they, too, should behave. Children also learn about the manner in which the world around them functions through the interactions of the members of the family with the world outside the household. This allows the child to understand more complex types of social interaction such as what goods the family needs, where the family must go to fulfill those needs, and what is needed to acquire those necessities (e.g., how much money is required to purchase an item).

1. Behavioral modeling, when related to child development within a family structure, is the manner in which children model their own behavior after the behavior of their parents and other people with whom they interact. Children learn what behavior is socially acceptable by mimicking the behavior of the people around them.
2. Consumer education is the process of teaching a person about the marketplace and its goods and services, the suppliers, and the various considerations associated with searching for goods and services. These concepts are critical for family members to learn so that they can survive in a consumer society.
3. Heritage is anything inherited from one's ancestors, including traditions, customs, or physical characteristics. The family conveys the traditions, customs, and social norms of the previous generation to the generations that follow.

Roles essential to the functioning of a healthy family

There are five major roles that are essential to the functioning of a healthy family. These roles are provision of necessities, development and education, emotional support, management of the family, and satisfaction of the married couple's needs. Individuals within the family need to provide necessities by creating income so that the family has access to food, clothing, and shelter. Family members need to teach not only customs, but also skills that will help the members of the family achieve academically and professionally. Families must provide emotional support for the family members during times of high stress. In addition, the family needs someone to take a leadership role and handle issues such as managing finances and maintaining the roles essential to the family's survival. The married couple has its own requirements, including basic necessities, sexual needs, and emotional needs that must be met for the family to continue functioning normally.

- 5 -

Role, role confusion, and role strain

A role is a collection of social rights, behaviors, and obligations that is assigned to a particular individual. For example, a mother's role might be that of a provider because she is out in the workforce earning an income for the family.

Role confusion occurs when an individual is uncertain of what role or roles he or she should play in a particular situation. For example, a nurse might run into a patient whom she took care of previously while out grocery shopping and be unsure of whether to act in a formal, nurse-to-patient manner or in an informal, friendly manner.

Role strain occurs when an individual is placed in a situation in which carrying out the duties of a certain role will prevent the individual from fulfilling his or her obligations of another role. For example, a working mother might be both caregiver and provider. If her child becomes ill, she cannot carry out both roles; she is forced to choose between working and caring for the sick child.

Marriage

Marriage is a union between two individuals that is often held as a legally binding contract in which the members of the union state their intention to live together and aid each other in maintaining a family. Even though couples who simply live together in the same household can constitute a family under the commonly used definition, the institution of marriage offers a level of stability to the family structure that is not present when an unmarried couple makes up the center of the family. This added stability is primarily a result of the societal, religious, and governmental recognition of the institution of marriage, which creates an expectation that the marriage—and ultimately the family—will remain intact. Although many married couples eventually separate and divorce, it is more difficult for a member of the marital couple to leave the family than it would be for a member of a couple who has no legal or societal obligation to remain together.

The married couple or, in some cases, the couple living together is the core of the family and therefore has a profound effect on the relationships and well-being of the family. If a marital couple is having difficulty in their relationship, and the stress of those difficulties becomes apparent, the rest of the family will most likely exhibit signs of stress. For example, if the marital couple is consistently seen fighting, or even if they just become withdrawn after a fight, other family members may react to the stress and become withdrawn, upset, or even hostile. On the other hand, marital couples who are not experiencing marital difficulties and who appear warm and affectionate will foster the same feelings of warmth and affection in the rest of the family.

Family

The primary purpose of a family is to ensure the survival of the family and to nurture the children. Families facilitate survival by sharing the work and tasks such as earning a living and taking care of the home. Family also provides emotional support to one another during stressful times. The family nurtures the children by offering social and emotional interaction, protecting them from potential danger, and educating them in social norms and customs. The family also provides the basic necessities required for the basic physical development of the children in the household, including food, clothing, shelter, and play.

- 6 -

A family is commonly considered a group of individuals related by birth, adoption, or marriage who reside together, usually for the purpose of raising children. However, a family can refer to any group of people who live together in the same household even if they are not related by blood or legal ties. This means that an unmarried couple who is living together or even a pair of roommates may still be considered a family. A single individual, though, is the opposite of a family because it is a person who lives alone and therefore does not regularly interact with relatives or other individuals within the household.

Family structures

The four major types of family structures are nuclear, extended, single-parent, and blended. Each of these structures is based on the idea that a family is a group of people who participate in raising the next generation. A nuclear family is the traditional concept of a family in which a mother, father, and their children live in the same household. An extended family is an expansion of the nuclear family that includes the mother, father, and their children as well as aunts, uncles, cousins, and grandparents. A single-parent structure is a family in which one parent is the only one in the home caring for the children. A blended family, also known as a stepfamily, is one in which a parent marries or remarries when he or she already has his or her own children, and there is a parent, stepparent, and one or more children living in the household.

The typical family structure in the United States has changed dramatically in recent years as the norm moves away from the nuclear family and toward the blended family. As more people divorce and remarry, blended families are becoming much more common. In this family structure, children are cared for by both biological and stepparents. This increase in the number of blended families, which were unheard of 50 years ago, has resulted in two substructures: simple and complex. In a simple stepfamily, only one of the individuals marrying has children before the marriage. In a complex stepfamily, both parents marrying have their own children before the marriage.

Family life cycle

There are commonly nine stages in the family life cycle. The first five stages are as follows: the bachelor stage, the newly married couple stage, full nest stage I, full nest stage II, and full nest stage III. The bachelor stage is the stage in which the individual is yet to be married, and the family has not yet been established. The second stage is the newly married couple stage in which two individuals have just married but do not have children. The third stage is the beginning of the three full nest stages, when the parents are beginning to raise children. During full nest stage I, the youngest child is under six. The fourth stage, full nest stage II, is when the youngest child is six or over. The fifth stage, full nest stage III, is the stage in which an older married couple has independent children.

The last four stages of the family life cycle are the empty nest I stage, the empty nest II stage, the solitary survivor in labor force stage, and the retired solitary survivor stage. During empty nest I stage, the head of the household is married and still in the labor force, but the couple has no children at home. Empty nest II stage is the same as empty nest I stage except that the head of the household has retired. The next stage, solitary survivor in labor force stage, occurs when one member of the couple has passed away, and the survivor must continue to work to support him or herself. The final stage, the retired solitary survivor stage, is the same as the solitary survivor in labor force stage except that the survivor has retired, and there are no longer any individuals living in the household who are still in the labor force.

Human Development and Parenting

Jean Piaget's theory of cognitive development

Piaget Play

Jean Piaget's theory of cognitive development theorizes that children will learn more effectively if they are allowed to actively adapt to the world around them through play and exploration rather than being taught skills and knowledge by others. Piaget's theory suggests that there are four major stages that children will go through as they begin to acquire new skills that will aid their ability to learn and process information independently. The four stages of cognitive development that Piaget identifies are the sensorimotor stage, which spans from ages zero to two; the preoperational stage, spanning from ages two to seven; the concrete operational stage for ages seven to 11; and the formal operational stage for ages 11 and up. Piaget's theory is important to the study of child development because it was the first theory that recognized that children can actively and effectively learn on their own rather than being dependent on another person for learning to occur.

The first stage of Piaget's theory of cognitive development, the sensorimotor stage, lasts from birth to age two. This is the period during which a child uses his or her senses of sight, hearing, and touch to learn about and explore elements of the world. Using these senses, children are able to discover new ways of solving simple problems such as using their hands to drop a block into a bucket and then remove it from the bucket. Another example is learning to use their eyes to find an object or person that has been hidden. As a result, it is also at this stage that a child begins to develop hand-eye coordination and the ability to reason out a method of achieving goals.

The second stage of Piaget's theory of cognitive development is the preoperational stage. It spans from ages two to seven. This is the stage in which children begin to use words, symbols, and pictures to describe what they have discovered about particular elements of the world around them. During this stage, children begin to develop an understanding of language, and they can focus their attention on a particular subject or object. Piaget theorized that children at this stage have a faulty sense of logic when attempting to understand certain concepts such as volume, mass, and number when some element is changed. For example, if a liquid is poured into a tall container, and then an equal amount of liquid is poured into a smaller but wider container, the children would believe that the taller container contains more liquid even though this obviously is not the case.

The third stage of Piaget's theory of cognitive development is the concrete operational stage occurring between ages seven and 11. It is the stage in which a child's thinking becomes more logical regarding concrete concepts. In this stage, children are capable of understanding concepts of mass, volume, and number. For example, they can understand that two containers of different shapes that each have the same amount of liquid poured into them still contain the same amount of liquid despite their differences in appearance. The child also begins to identify and organize objects according to shape, size, and color. The child will not be able to understand more abstract concepts such as those found in calculus or algebra, however, until he or she reaches the formal operational stage of development.

The fourth and final stage of Piaget's theory of cognitive development, the formal operational stage, starts at age 11 and continues until the end of an individual's life. During this stage, an individual understands more abstract concepts and develops a logical way of thinking about those concepts. In other words, an individual begins to understand ideas that are less concrete or absolute and that cannot necessarily be backed up by physical evidence or observation such as morality, advanced mathematics, and a person's state of being. It is also within this stage of development that individuals can understand all the variables in a problem and are able to determine most, if not all, the possible solutions to a problem rather than just the most obvious solutions. This stage is never truly completed; it continues throughout a person's life as the individual develops and improves his or her ability to think abstractly.

Later researchers have challenged Piaget's theory of cognitive development because studies indicate that Piaget may have underestimated the abilities of younger children to learn and understand various concepts. Piaget's theory indicates that younger children are unable to understand certain concrete and abstract thoughts early within their development even if another individual teaches the child. However, this notion has been disproved. Research shows that young children can be taught how to handle and understand problems that Piaget believed only older children would be able to comprehend. Researchers have also challenged Piaget's theory because studies indicate that if a younger child is given a task like one an older child might receive, but the difficulty of the task is adjusted to compensate for age, the younger child would actually understand the concept more effectively. Piaget's theory is still important, though, because it presents the importance of active learning in a child's development. Notably, Piaget's theory ignores many of the benefits of adult learning.

Abraham Maslow's hierarchy of human needs

Abraham Maslow theorized that there are five types of human needs that, if arranged in order of importance, form a pyramid. Maslow maintained that individuals would not be able to focus on the upper layers of the hierarchy until they were first able to meet the needs at the lower layers. The first layer of the pyramid represents the physiological needs, which are the basic needs required for an individual's survival such as food, water, breathable air, and sleep. The second layer of the pyramid represents the safety needs, which are the elements that an individual needs to feel a sense of security such as having a job, good health, and a safe place to live. The third layer of the pyramid corresponds to the love and belonging needs, which are needed to form social relationships such as those with friends, family, and intimate loved ones.

The fourth layer of Maslow's hierarchy of human needs is the esteem layer, which represents the individual's need to respect him or herself and be respected and accepted by others. The fifth and top layer of the pyramid is the self-actualization layer. It represents the individual's need for morality, creativity, and trust. Maslow theorized that individuals could survive without reaching the higher levels of the pyramid but that would feel a sense of anxiousness if these needs were not met. Maslow also believed that individuals who reached the higher levels of the pyramid did not receive any tangible benefit from meeting these needs other than a feeling of fulfillment and the motivation to fulfill needs higher on the pyramid.

Maslow later added two additional layers above the self-actualization layer of the pyramid. These are the cognitive layer and the aesthetic layer. The cognitive layer is the layer that represents an individual's need to acquire and ultimately understand both abstract and concrete knowledge. The aesthetic layer, which became the final layer in later versions of the pyramid, is the layer that represents the individual's need to discover, create, and experience beauty and art. Maslow later theorized that if an individual was unable to meet the needs of any given layer of the pyramid, those needs could become neurotic needs. Such needs are compulsions that, if satisfied, would not facilitate the individual's health or growth.

Erikson's theory of psychosocial development

Erik Erikson's theory of psychosocial development breaks the process of human development into eight stages necessary for healthy functioning. The eight stages Erikson identified are infancy, younger years, early childhood, middle childhood, adolescence, early adulthood, middle adulthood, and later adulthood. During each of these stages, individuals must overcome a developmental obstacle, which Erikson called a crisis, to be able to progress and face the crises of later stages. If an individual is not able to overcome one of the crises along the way, later crises will be more difficult for him or her to overcome. Erikson's theory also maintains that individuals who are unable to successfully pass through a particular crisis will likely encounter that same crisis again.

The first stage of Erikson's theory of psychosocial development is infancy, which spans from birth to 12 months. In this stage, a child is presented with the crisis of trust versus mistrust. Although everyone struggles with this crisis throughout their lives, a child needs to be able to realize the concept of trust and the elements of certainty. For example, a child learns that if his or her parents leave the room, they aren't going to abandon the child forever. If a child is unable to realize the concept of trust because of traumatic life events, such as abandonment, the child may become withdrawn and avoid interaction with the rest of society.

The second stage of Erikson's theory of psychosocial development is the younger years stage, which covers ages one to three. In this stage, a child is faced with the crisis of autonomy versus shame and doubt. The child is presented with the need to become independent and learn skills such as using the toilet without assistance. If the child is able to overcome this crisis, he or she will gain the sense of self-pride necessary to continue fostering the child's growing need for independence. If, however, the child is unable to overcome this crisis and cannot establish his or her own independence, the child will develop feelings of shame and doubt about his or her ability to function without assistance.

The third stage of Erikson's theory of psychosocial development is the early childhood stage, spanning ages three to five. In this stage, a child is faced with the crisis of initiative versus guilt. The child is presented with the need to discover the ambition necessary to continue functioning independently. This stage is strongly linked with the moral development of the child as he or she begins to use make-believe play to explore the kind of person he or she wants to become in the future. If children are unable to explore their ambitions or if they are expected to function with too much self-control, they will develop feelings of guilt as they begin to see their ambitions, dreams, and goals as unattainable or inappropriate.

The fourth stage of Erikson's theory of psychosocial development is the middle childhood stage, which covers ages six to 10. In this stage, a child is faced with the crisis of industry

- 11 -

versus inferiority and is presented with the need to develop the ability to complete productive tasks such as schoolwork and working in groups. If children are unable to learn how to work effectively, either alone or in a group, they will develop a sense of inferiority as a result of their inability to complete the tasks set before them that their peers are capable of completing. For example, if a child is regularly unable to complete their homework because the child does not understand the material while the rest of the child's peers are not having difficulty, this can lead the child to develop a sense of inferiority.

The fifth stage of Erikson's theory of psychosocial development is the adolescence stage, which covers ages 11 to 18. In this stage, the child is faced with the crisis of identity versus role confusion. During this stage, the child attempts to find his or her place in society and identify future goals and the skills and values necessary to achieve those goals. At this stage, the child also becomes more aware of how people perceive him or her and becomes concerned with those perceptions. If the child is unable to determine what future goals he or she is interested in pursuing, it can lead to confusion about what roles the child will play when he or she reaches adulthood.

The sixth stage of Erikson's theory of psychosocial development is the early adulthood stage, which covers ages 18 to 34. In this stage, the young adult is concerned with the crisis of intimacy versus isolation in which an individual needs to begin establishing intimate relationships with others. If an adult is unable to form intimate relationships with others, perhaps because of disappointing relationships in the past, this person will become more withdrawn and will isolate him or herself from others. Isolation can prove to be a perilous problem in the development of a healthy adult, as it prevents the individual from forming lasting relationships. The lack of social interaction can also lead to severe personality flaws, which may hinder the development of future relationships.

The seventh stage of Erikson's theory of psychosocial development is the middle adulthood stage, occurring between the ages of 35 and 60. In this stage, an adult becomes aware of the crisis of generativity versus stagnation in which the individual is concerned with continuing his or her genetic line before it is too late. Generativity refers to the ability to produce offspring and then nurture, guide, and prepare that offspring for future life. At the same time, however, generativity in this context also refers to any act that gives something of value to the next generation such as teaching children how to read. If an individual is unable to contribute to the next generation in some form, the individual will feel a sense of failure resulting from stagnation, which is simply a lack of accomplishment.

The last stage of Erikson's eight stages of psychosocial development is the later adulthood stage, which is the period that starts at age 60 and extends to the end of one's life. In this stage, an individual is confronted with the crisis of ego integrity versus despair. During this time, an adult begins to examine the course of his or her life by reflecting on the kind of person that he or she has been. If the adult feels that he or she has had a meaningful life and has accomplished something during it, this will lead to a strong sense of integrity. However, if the individual is unhappy with the way he or she has acted, this person will experience despair and will fear death as the absolute end of further achievement.

Familial roles

Fifty years ago, women were the primary caretakers of the family's children, and they were in charge of maintaining the household while men worked to provide for the family. This has changed, however, because of the drastic increase in the number of women entering the workforce since that time. This is partially because it has become more difficult for families to subsist on one income alone. Both members of the marital couple are often forced to work to provide for the family, which can make it difficult when trying to balance the responsibilities of caretaker and provider. Men, who were once the primary providers for the family, are still out in the workforce, but their spouses have joined them, and both individuals have to find ways to make the time to care for the family's children.

Nature versus nurture

The concept of nature versus nurture is the idea that of all a person's traits, some result from his or her genetic heritage, and some result from his or her environment. In this context, nature refers to any trait that an individual is born with, or has acquired through genes. Nurture may be seen as the opposite of nature; it refers to any trait that an individual learns from the environment. Nurture often refers specifically to the environment created by the parents of the child, but it can refer to any environmental condition that affects the development of the child. The concept of nature versus nurture is important because it shows that individuals inherit some of their traits from their parents, but they also develop many of their traits from their environment.

Genetic and environmental traits

Research has shown that some traits that are almost completely genetic include eye color, blood type, and most diseases. In most cases, genetics also determines one's risk of future diseases, vision, and vision impairments. Religion and language, on the other hand, are examples of traits that researchers have proven to be almost completely environmental. These traits are all linked to specific genes or to specific environmental factors, but most traits are actually a result of both environmental and genetic influences. Traits such as height, weight, and skin color are all examples of traits that are influenced by both an individual's genes and his or her environment.

Havinghurst's developmental task concept

The developmental task concept is a theory of human development established by Robert Havinghurst that states that there are certain tasks each individual needs to go through at points during his or her life to continue developing into a happy and successful adult. These tasks, separated into three groups by their causes, are tasks resulting from physical maturation, personal causes, and societal pressures. A child learning to crawl is an example of a task that becomes necessary as the child matures physically. An individual learning basic first aid because he or she is interested in becoming an EMT is an example of a personal cause. An example of a task resulting from societal pressure is a child learning to behave appropriately in a store.

The first three major age periods identified by Havinghurst in his developmental task concept are infancy and early childhood, middle childhood, and adolescence. Infancy and early childhood is the period from ages zero to five, and it consists of tasks such as learning to walk, talk, and eat solid foods as well as learning right from wrong. Middle childhood is the period of development from ages six to 12 that includes tasks such as learning to get along with others, moral values, and skills and knowledge required for day-to-day living. Adolescence is the period from ages 13 to 18, and it requires tasks that include learning

- 13 -

how to relate with members of the opposite sex, learning the social role of one's gender in society, and preparing for life after childhood.

The last three major age periods identified by Havinghurst in his developmental task concept are early adulthood, middle adulthood, and later maturity. Early adulthood is the period of life from ages 19 to 29, and it is the age range where tasks such as starting a long-term relationship, finding a career, and starting a family are required. Middle adulthood is the period from ages 30 to 60 that includes tasks such as finding adult recreational activities, achieving in one's chosen career, and helping one's teenage children become healthy and happy adults. Later maturity is the period from ages 61 to the end of a person's life. This period consists of tasks such as adjusting to the death of a spouse, adjusting to the effects of old age, and finding people in one's peer group to interact with.

Early childhood intervention and intellectual giftedness

Early childhood intervention is the process by which children who are experiencing or showing signs of developmental difficulties are diagnosed and treated early to allow them to continue developing in the best manner possible. Early childhood intervention services usually take place before the child reaches school age because studies indicate that the earlier a child who is experiencing difficulties receives special education, the more effective that education will ultimately be.

Intellectual giftedness refers to children who are born with a significantly higher than average IQ and who are capable of learning concepts and information much more quickly than other children their age. Even though intellectual giftedness is an asset to the child, the child often requires education that is adjusted for the speed at which the child can learn. Otherwise, the child will become bored, frustrated, isolated, and may begin to underachieve.

Substance abuse

Substance abuse is a disorder in which an individual begins to overuse or becomes dependent on a particular drug or a group of drugs that ultimately has a negative impact on his or her health and human development. Substance abuse, especially when the individual becomes addicted to or dependent on the drug, can affect the individual's ability to interact both socially and physically. His or her ability to communicate intelligibly or even to complete relatively simple tasks can be severely hindered. After an individual has become chemically dependent on a particular drug, his or her body develops a physical need for the drug, and the individual will experience the effects of withdrawal if he or she is unable to meet that need. However, substance abuse not only affects a person by causing health problems, it also severely hinders an individual's ability for social development, as the individual often has difficulty improving social skills because of his or her inability to control behavior, actions, and even basic speech.

Teenage pregnancy

Teenage pregnancy can be defined as the act of a woman expecting a child prior to her twentieth birthday or, in some areas, prior to her being considered a legal adult. Teenage pregnancy can have a significant number of physical, social, economic, and psychological effects. Studies show that women who become pregnant as teenagers have a significantly higher chance of giving birth to the child prematurely, a higher risk of the child being born

- 14 -

at an unhealthy weight, and a higher risk of complications during pregnancy, especially when the mother is under the age of 15. It has also been shown that teenage mothers are more likely to drop out of high school and are even more likely never to finish college. This can make it much more difficult for a teenage mother to find a job, especially if she is the sole caretaker of her child. Also, children born to teenage mothers have been shown to be at higher risk for behavioral problems and often have more difficulty functioning in school.

The two primary ways that the risk of teenage pregnancy can be reduced are through the promotion of contraceptive use or abstinence and through the promotion of social interaction between teenagers and their parents. The best way to reduce the risk of teenage pregnancy is to abstain from intercourse, but the use of a contraceptive, even though it does not guarantee that a teenager will not become pregnant, can greatly reduce the chances of pregnancy when used correctly. Studies have also shown that teenagers who have regular, open communication with their parents are more likely to wait to have intercourse until later in their lives. However, regardless of what precautions are used, the risk of teenage pregnancy cannot be eliminated completely, as there is always the risk of contraceptives failing or the risk that a teenager may become a rape victim.

Maintaining a stable and effective support system before and after a child is born is the most important factor for a teenage mother to function and raise her child in a healthy fashion. Studies have shown that most of the physical effects on the children of teenage pregnancy are a result of malnutrition and poor prenatal care. Both of these factors can be greatly reduced or eliminated if the young mother has help from parents or outside resources that teach her what to eat and where to get appropriate care. Because teenage parents almost always lack the resources and the life experience necessary to both supply and care for the child, a strong support system is essential in helping the mother financially and in raising the child.

Teenage suicide

There are a number of factors that increase the risk of teenage suicide, but studies indicate that a teenager's history, emotional and physical health, social pressures, and access to the methods necessary to carry out a suicide are the most influential factors. If a teenager has attempted suicide, has a history of drug or alcohol abuse, a history of depression or other mental illness, or another family member has committed suicide or been abused, the teenager's risk of suicide increases. Physical illness, religious or cultural pressures, and other suicides in the community can also lead to an increased risk of suicide among teenagers. Finally, if the teenager has access to guns, knives, drugs, or any other means of taking his or her own life, the teenager may be at heightened risk for suicide.

Nutrition and Wellness

Anorexia, bulimia, and obesity

Anorexia and bulimia are very similar disorders, but the one major difference between the two conditions is control. An individual suffering from anorexia is usually already below a healthy weight, still perceives that his or her own weight is unacceptable, and therefore attempts to lower that weight further by limiting food intake. Bulimic individuals, on the other hand, have no sense of control over their eating habits. They instead eat excessively and then attempt to overcompensate for their excessive food intake. In short, individuals suffering from anorexia are usually below what would normally be considered a healthy weight for their age and size and attempt to control their eating to reduce their weight further. Bulimic individuals, however, are usually above a healthy weight as they have no control over their own eating.

Anorexia is an eating disorder in which an individual views his or her own body as being overweight, even though he or she is not, which causes the person to have an extreme, unfounded fear of gaining additional weight. This fear can lead individuals to use desperate and unhealthy methods to reduce their weight below what would normally be healthy. These methods include deliberate vomiting, limiting their food intake, exercising excessively without eating enough food, and using medications to flush their system. Anorexia is commonly found to affect young women, specifically during adolescence. It can pose a serious risk to an individual's health as the obsessive attempts to reduce body weight can affect the health of the heart, brain, immune system, muscles, and other organs. Anorexia can be extremely difficult to treat as it is a complicated psychological condition, but it has been shown that psychotherapy may be able to help the individual overcome the inaccurate perceptions she or he has regarding his or her own body.

Bulimia is an eating disorder, similar to anorexia, in which an individual views his or her own body as being unattractive or overweight, but lacks the ability to control his or her own eating. Bulimic individuals regularly eat an unhealthily large amount of food and then attempt to flush their systems to prevent themselves from gaining additional weight. Some of the methods individuals suffering from bulimia might use to flush food from their systems include deliberate vomiting, excessive exercise, and using diet pills, laxatives, ipecac, and other medications. Bulimia is most commonly found in women, especially younger women from ages 12 to 19, and can have a significant impact on the health of the individual. It can cause problems such as anemia, weakness, muscle and heart problems, dehydration, malnutrition, damage to the stomach, and a wide range of other problems. Bulimia is difficult to treat, but a combination of group psychotherapy and low doses of anti-psychotic medications have been shown to help.

Obesity is a condition of the body where the individual has increased his or her own body weight significantly beyond what is normally considered healthy, usually by excessive eating. Obesity occurs because the individual takes in more food than his or her body can actually use, and the excess food is stored as fat. Overeating is the primary cause of obesity, but obesity can also be tied to family history, genetic factors, stress and lack of sleep, various illnesses and conditions, and many other causes. An individual who is obese is at a significantly higher risk for certain health problems, including problems with the heart, stomach, muscles, lungs, skin, nervous system, and many other areas of the body. The best way to treat obesity is through a well-balanced diet that eliminates excessive food intake and a rigorous exercise program. In extreme cases, individuals may also use medication or even surgery to help lower their weight.

Unfortunately, there is no known way of completely eliminating the risk of an individual developing an eating-related condition such as anorexia, bulimia, and obesity, but it has been shown that some methods may significantly lower the risk of developing these conditions. The best way to reduce the risk of developing eating disorders or becoming obese is for parents to interact more with their children and make sure that they are teaching them good eating habits early on. It is also important that parents attempt to build-up the self-esteem of their children through interactions that show high esteem in both the parents and child. Children who have been taught good eating habits by their parents and who have been taught to have high self-esteem have been shown to eat more carefully, and therefore are at a significantly lower risk of becoming obese or developing eating disorders such as anorexia and bulimia.

Diabetes

Diabetes is a disease that prevents the body from producing or using a hormone called insulin, which the body needs to process sugar and use it as energy for the cells of the body. Since an individual with diabetes cannot produce insulin or cannot use what is produced, the body is unable to appropriately use the sugar that the cells need to survive. Instead the sugar builds up in the body, leading to a high sugar concentration in the blood, which is a condition known as hyperglycemia. Diabetes can lead to a series of dangerous health problems including the potential failure of the heart, kidneys, nerves, and eyes as well as conditions such as high blood pressure, blindness, poor healing of wounds, and many other dangerous conditions. There is currently no cure for diabetes, but the negative effects of diabetes can be controlled through careful monitoring of blood sugar levels, the use of a specific diet to maintain the individual's blood sugar, and through the use of certain drugs and/or insulin shots.

The three types of diabetes are type 1, type 2, and gestational diabetes. Type 1 diabetes is a form of diabetes in which the individual's own immune system mistakes the beta cells of the pancreas, which are the cells responsible for producing insulin, as being harmful and therefore attacks and destroys them. Type 1 diabetes prevents the individual from actually producing insulin. It is treated primarily through the use of a carefully constructed diet and insulin injections or the use of an insulin pump. Both type 2 diabetes and gestational diabetes are conditions in which the individual is either unable to produce enough insulin for the body or the cells of the body are unable to use the insulin correctly. Type 2 and gestational diabetes can both be treated through the use of a carefully monitored diet along with medication to help the body use the insulin appropriately. The only major difference between type 2 diabetes and gestational diabetes is that gestational diabetes occurs specifically due to hormones present during pregnancy.

There is currently no way to completely prevent an individual from developing diabetes, but the risk of developing certain forms of diabetes can be reduced. The risk of type 2 diabetes and gestational diabetes can be reduced by eating a more healthy diet high in fiber and whole grains, exercising regularly, and lowering the amount of high-fat foods that the individual eats. It has also been suggested that the risk of a mother developing gestational diabetes may be reduced through breast-feeding as it allows the mother to release some of the excess hormones present in her body as a result of the pregnancy. The risk of type 2 and gestational diabetes can be reduced, but there is, unfortunately, no known way of preventing type 1 diabetes, as researchers know very little about the exact causes of the disease.

Hypertension

Hypertension is a condition in which an individual's blood pressure is regularly higher than the range that is normally acceptable. The blood pressure of a healthy individual should be somewhere between 90/50 and 120/80, and anything over 140/90 is considered to be a high blood pressure. Anything between 120/80 and 140/90 is considered to be prehypertension, in which the individual does not yet have dangerously high blood pressure, but is at significant risk of developing hypertension if steps are not taken to lower the blood pressure. Hypertension can significantly impact virtually every part of the body as the increased force of the blood against the artery walls can severely damage the body's organs, including the heart, brain, eyes, and kidneys if it goes untreated. Usually there are no apparent symptoms associated with hypertension, but individuals with extremely high blood pressure might experience headaches, vomiting, and difficulty seeing clearly.

Hypertension can usually be treated through the use of a low-salt and low-fat diet along with exercise to bring the individual's blood pressure back down to a reasonable level. People who are being treated for hypertension are usually also advised to stop smoking and drinking to excess, unless it is believed that ceasing these activities will actually put too much additional stress on the individual's body. Persons with significantly higher blood pressures are also often prescribed medication that will help reduce their blood pressure further. There is no way to completely eliminate the risk of hypertension and some factors, including age, race, and family history, can make the individual more predisposed to developing hypertension. However, there are certain factors that individuals can eliminate from their daily activities to significantly lower their risk of developing hypertension. These activities include excessive drinking, smoking, regularly consuming high-salt foods, regular involvement in high-stress activities, and other similar factors that put additional stress on the body.

Vitamin A

Vitamin A, also known as retinol, is important because it aids in bone growth, skin health, and the ability to reproduce. Vitamin A also promotes eye health and aids in the production of tears, which prevents the eyes from drying out and washes away bacteria that might cause infections. A vitamin A deficiency can cause the eyes to deteriorate and may lead to conditions such as night blindness, also known as nyctalopia, in which an individual has difficulty seeing in low light environments. Common sources of vitamin A include carrots, sweet potatoes, pumpkins, spinach, beef, pork, chicken, eggs, and broccoli. Both men and women require similar amounts of vitamin A for their bodies to function normally, but men usually require slightly more than women do.

Vitamin B12

B12, also known as cyanocobalamin, is important because it is necessary for the production of blood cells and aids in maintaining the health of the nervous system. A severe lack of B12 within the body can lead to a variety of conditions including megaloblastic anemia, a condition in which the red blood cells have less hemoglobin and therefore have more difficulty functioning properly. A significant lack of B12 can also lead to severe problems with the nervous system because the lack of B12 causes the disintegration and death of nerve cells. Individuals who lack significant quantities of B12 may develop symptoms such as numbness, tingling, and difficulty with muscle control. Some common sources of B12 include chicken, beef, pork, liver, fish, shellfish, certain breakfast cereals, milk, cheese, eggs, and yogurt. Vegetarians may have difficulty getting enough B12 since the primary sources of B12 are meat products, but B12 supplements and multivitamins can be a good option as well.

Vitamin C

Vitamin C, also known as ascorbic acid, is important because it helps protect the health of the skin, bones, teeth, cartilage, and blood vessels. Vitamin C protects these areas of the body primarily by acting as an antioxidant that helps reduce the negative effects that oxygen reactions within the body can have on the cells. Vitamin C is also necessary in the production of collagen, which is a protein necessary for skin and cartilage health. Significant vitamin C deficiencies can result in a number of serious health problems including a disorder known as scurvy, in which the body lacks the collagen it requires to maintain the health of the skin. Scurvy ultimately leads to the formation of liver spots on the skin and gums, and can also cause bleeding from all the body's mucous membranes including the nose, lips, ears and other areas. Common sources of vitamin C include strawberries, oranges, lemons, limes, mangos, grapes, broccoli, potatoes, spinach, liver, and milk.

Vitamin E

Vitamin E, also known as tocopherol, is important primarily because it aids in maintaining proper brain function and eye health. It has also been suggested that vitamin E may help reduce the risk of cancer, cataracts, heart disease, and other health conditions as well as helping treat patients that have Parkinson's or Alzheimer's Disease. A significant vitamin E deficiency can result in muscle weakness, blindness, and neurological problems as a result of the body transmitting nerve impulses incorrectly. Common sources of vitamin E include peanuts, hazelnuts, coconuts, corn, asparagus, carrots, tomatoes, fish, peanut butter, and vegetable oils. There are also many multivitamins and supplements that supply vitamin E, but some studies have shown that some synthetic vitamins and supplements may actually be significantly less beneficial or even have a negative impact on the individual when taken in large doses. However, both men and women do require vitamin E, in similar amounts, to continue functioning normally.

Iron

Iron is important because it aids in the proper functioning of virtually all the muscles and organs. Iron also allows the body to form hemoglobin, which is a protein in red blood cells that carries oxygen throughout the body. If an individual does not have enough iron in his or her diet, anemia, a condition in which the body is unable to produce hemoglobin, can result. The body may also be unable to produce additional red blood cells if there is a lack of iron, and the individual will be more likely to become fatigued and develop other symptoms and conditions. Common sources of iron include oatmeal, spaghetti, whole wheat bread, sunflower seeds, broccoli, green beans, beets, peas, potatoes, green leafy vegetables, beef, pork, and chicken. Women usually require more iron than men do partially because of the regular blood loss associated with menstruation.

Fiber

Fiber is an important part of an individual's diet because it helps with bowel movements, digestion, and immune responses. Fiber has also been shown to lower blood cholesterol, help prevent obesity, lower the risk of certain types of cancer including colon cancer, and lower the risk of type 2 diabetes. A significant lack of fiber in an individual's diet can lead to symptoms such as constipation and slower digestion and can cause an individual to have a higher risk of developing certain diseases. Some common sources of fiber include certain breakfast cereals, oatmeal, whole-wheat bread, beans, apples, pears, strawberries, bananas, potatoes, onions, and green beans. Both men and women require similar amounts of fiber to continue functioning properly.

Protein

Protein is important to the functioning of a healthy individual because it is necessary for the body to produce the amino acids it needs to continue functioning. Most of the amino acids that the body needs are already present in the body, but certain amino acids, known as essential amino acids, can only be produced when the body digests protein. A severe lack of protein is usually caused by malnutrition and can lead to reduced brain function, intellectual disabilities, and an overall weakening of the immune system due to a decrease in the number of white blood cells. It has also been suggested that a significant lack of protein may lead to conditions such as kwashiorkor, which causes significant weight loss, thinning and discolored hair, swelling of the organs, and weakens the responses of the immune system. Some common sources of protein include chicken, beef, wheat, rice, milk, cheese, eggs, peas, beans, peanuts, and peanut butter.

Calcium

Calcium is important to the development and maintenance of bones and teeth, since a lack of calcium can result in osteoporosis and other bone problems. Calcium is also important to the production of lymph, which is a fluid similar to interstitial fluid that aids in the overall operation of the body, specifically the immune system. Common sources of calcium are milk, cheese, honey, eggs, orange juice, oranges, broccoli, rutabagas, almonds and other nuts. Calcium can also be obtained through supplements and multivitamins, which can be a good source for people who are allergic to dairy products or have a significant calcium deficiency. Both men and women require similar amounts of calcium, but the amount of calcium required increases as an individual ages.

RDA and RDI

RDA stands for recommended dietary allowance, which is the amount of each vitamin, mineral, or other nutrient that health professionals believe an individual needs to receive daily in order to stay healthy. The RDA has been replaced by the now more commonly used RDI or reference daily intake. The RDI is similar to the RDA, but does not recommend different nutrient intakes based on gender and age as the RDA does. The RDI is used to determine the RDV, or recommended daily value, which is printed on virtually every food product in the United States and Canada to inform consumers of the nutritional value, or the lack thereof, that each product offers. These recommended daily values are usually based on a 2000-calorie diet, and since the RDI recommends the same nutrient intake for everyone, there is no difference shown between the intakes necessary for individuals of different age groups or genders. Both the RDA and RDI are important because they allow consumers to determine which foods are best for their diet.

Low activity and high activity individuals

A low activity individual is usually considered to be anyone who does not exercise regularly and gets less than 30 minutes of exercise on any given day. A high activity individual is usually considered to be anyone who exercises regularly and gets at least 30 to 60 minutes of exercise 4 to 5 times a week. An individual can also be considered high activity if he or she is in a profession that is physically intense such as warehouse workers, moving company workers, gym teachers, etc. Individuals who exercise more than 30 minutes at a time, but do so only once or twice a week are usually considered mid-level activity persons rather than high or low activity individuals.

Vitamins and daily number of calories that a healthy individual needs

Nutritional needs change in a variety of ways as an individual ages, but the major changes involve which vitamins and the number of calories the body requires to keep functioning. Young children usually require around 1000 to 1500 calories a day, but the amount of calories a child requires increases as the child grows. Young teens usually require somewhere between 1600 and 2200 calories a day, depending on their gender and other factors. Individuals entering young adulthood usually require between 2000 and 2400 calories a day. However, after a person reaches age 30, the calorie requirement begins to decrease and continues to do so as they get older. People also require progressively more Vitamins A, C, and E as well as iron and fiber as they age. Individuals over age 50 also require significantly more calcium.

Daily calorie and nutritional requirements of a healthy individual

An individual that is more active requires more calories than a person who is less active. A young active child usually requires about the same number of calories as a less active child, but the difference between the calorie needs increases substantially as the children grow. Active young teens require 1600 to 2600 calories, depending on gender and other factors, and active individuals entering young adulthood usually require between 2000 and 3200 calories. As these age ranges show, the calorie needs of an active individual is usually between 400 – 800 calories higher than a less active person. Active people also require more protein than less active individuals, but usually require similar amounts of Vitamins A, C, and E as well as iron and fiber.

Cholesterol

Cholesterol is a lipid, a type of fat that the body uses to produce both new cells and bile, a substance secreted by the liver that helps the body digest fat. Although the body requires a certain amount of cholesterol to continue functioning normally, excessive amounts of cholesterol can lead to heart and circulatory problems, including a condition known as atherosclerosis, a dangerous condition in which arteries are clogged by deposits of cholesterol. Clogged arteries can cause a variety of other serious problems, such as heart attacks and strokes, because the heart, brain, and many other vital organs cannot receive enough blood to function properly. One of the best ways to avoid too much cholesterol is to stay away from foods that contain high concentrations of saturated fats. Some examples of foods that are high in cholesterol and saturated fats are beef, pork, eggs, milk, butter, cheese, and most snack foods. Some examples of foods that are low in cholesterol and saturated fats include oatmeal, fish, rice, and most fruits and vegetables.

Carbohydrates

Carbohydrates, also known as saccharides, are a group of simple and complex sugars and starches that form an important class of foods in an individual's nutritional needs by supplying energy for the body. Such carbohydrates as the sugar glucose are transported throughout the body via the bloodstream and broken down into energy that keeps the body functioning. Carbohydrates are also important in the function and regulation of the body's immune system and reproductive system. In addition, because carbohydrates aid a person's blood in clotting effectively, they play an essential role in the body's ability to heal. Although many of the body's functions that carbohydrates play a role in can be carried out by proteins and fats as well, carbohydrates are easier for the body to digest and contain less cholesterol than proteins and saturated fats. Examples of foods that are high in carbohydrates include bread, beans, cereals, pasta, potatoes, and rice.

Fats

Fats are important to the healthy functioning of the body because they allow certain vitamins, including vitamins A, D, E, and K, to be digested and absorbed by the body. These fat-soluble vitamins can be broken down and used by the body only when enough fat is present. In addition, a lack of certain fats in an individual can lead to other vitamin deficiencies. Fats also help maintain the body's temperature; help promote hair, skin, and overall cell health; protect the body's organs; help protect against some diseases; and act as a means of storing energy for the body to use later. However, an excessive amount of fat in the body can adversely affect an individual's health, as an abundance of saturated fats and trans fats can greatly increase the cholesterol level in the blood, which in turn increases an individual's risk of certain heart conditions and other health problems. Some foods that individuals may want to avoid eating in excess because they are high in fat include butter, cream, cheese, lard, milk, and snack foods.

Iodine

Relatively small amounts of iodine are important to an individual's health because the element iodine is necessary for the production of thyroid hormones, which the body needs to function normally. A lack of iodine in an individual's diet or an excessive amount of iodine in the body can lead to a variety of symptoms and conditions including depression, fatigue, mental slowness or intellectual disability, excessive weight gain, and goiter, which is an enlargement of the thyroid gland characterized by an extremely swollen neck. Iodine deficiencies are fairly uncommon in the United States and other developed countries because most of the salt used in cooking has been treated with iodine to make sure that individuals ingest enough iodine on a daily basis. Other foods that have high concentrations of iodine include fish, kelp, and most dairy products.

Ethics and religion

An individual's religious, moral, and ethical beliefs can play a large part in his or her diet because some beliefs can result in the exclusion of certain foods. Ethical and moral considerations such as preventing animal cruelty or showing disapproval of environmentally unfriendly practices used to acquire certain types of food can lead some individuals to reduce the amount of certain foods they consume, such as meat, or eliminate those foods from their diet completely. For example, many individuals who choose to be vegetarians or vegans usually do so to avoid supporting what they believe to be the unethical slaughter of animals. Religious considerations can also determine a person's dietary choices, as some religions dictate what sort of foods the members of that faith can consume. People practicing Judaism, for instance, can consume only kosher foods, which are foods that conform to a series of guidelines established by the faith and include restrictions related to how an animal was slaughtered, what type of animal was slaughtered, and who prepared the food.

Ethnicity

Ethnicity can play an important role in the foods that an individual includes in his or her diet because people living in different regions of the world usually have different customs regarding the foods that they eat and have different foods commonly available as well. For example, individuals who live in a country like Japan that has easy access to waters suitable for fishing will typically consume significantly more fish than individuals who live in countries that are landlocked. Individuals who have immigrated to another country or who are descendents of immigrants will often include foods in their diet that are traditional foods from their native countries even if those foods are not easily accessible in their new home. People in some regions may include foods in their diets that are not based on how readily available a particular food is, but rather are based on the culture's customary eating habits, as seen in France, where the population as a whole tends to eat foods that are fresh rather than processed.

Food

Food is essential for the health of an individual, because it satisfies an individual's nutritional needs. Additionally, food provides many people some degree of psychological satisfaction as well. Food is a basic necessity for the successful functioning of an individual; therefore, the body makes a person aware of its need for food by creating a feeling of hunger in him or her. When the individual satisfies this hunger by consuming various foods, the body releases hormones that result in the person's feeling a sensation of being full, an indication that the body's need for sustenance has been assuaged. Certain types of foods satisfy an individual's hunger more effectively than other foods. Foods that are high in fiber, protein, and water usually will make an individual feel more satiated, or full. If an individual's body lacks a specific type of nutrient, the body will cause that person to experience a craving for foods that will satisfy that particular nutritional need.

Planning a nutritional meal for a group

Individuals or organizations that are planning to prepare a nutritionally-sound meal for a group of people should first decide what the nutritional goals of the meal are. Once these goals have been established, the individual or organization should continue the planning

- 23 -

Goals, research, plan time and cost, method
of order, handling, technique, prepare

process by researching which foods will best satisfy these goals without exceeding the available time and resource limits. The individual or organization should then put together a written meal plan that details what foods will be included, the average time it takes to prepare and cook each of these meals, and the cost associated with the preparation of these meals. The individual or organization should then determine the best method of preparing food for these meals, including which foods should be prepared first, the best way to handle or prepare the foods to minimize the risk of illness, and what techniques can be used to reduce the cooking time. Finally, the individual or organization can prepare the meal according to the plan that has been established.

Reducing the amount of time it takes to prepare a meal

Some of the methods that can be used to reduce the time it takes to prepare a meal include keeping the cooking equipment clean and organized, making sure frozen products are thawed ahead of time, preparing foods that have long cooking times beforehand, and preparing foods in order of their cooking times. By keeping the cooking area and the necessary cooking utensils clean, organized, and easily accessible, individuals or organizations can make sure that the time they have available is used as efficiently as possible. Along with thawing products beforehand, preparing foods that require long cooking times ahead of time and re-heating them later can also greatly reduce the amount of time it takes to prepare a meal. Preparing foods according to their cooking times, from longest to shortest, also greatly reduces preparation time because the individual or organization can prepare other foods for the meal while the foods that take the longest are already cooking.

Choosing what foods to prepare for a meal

An individual or organization that is deciding what foods to prepare for a meal should consider the food's nutritional value, the time it takes to prepare each food, the number of people to be served, and the cost of preparing each food. Each food has its own cooking time and offers different nutrients, so it is important that whoever is preparing the meal chooses to serve foods that satisfy people's nutritional goals without exceeding his or her time constraints for cooking the meal. Since most individuals or organizations will likely have a budgeted amount of money for the meal, they must consider the number of people to be served and how much each food costs to prepare. If the cost is too high, some meals may not be practical to serve to large groups of people. For example, if an individual or organization is interested in serving a good source of protein for a meal, steak might be a good option for a small group of people but would probably be too expensive for a larger group.

Food that might be found in the marketplace

The two primary types of food that an individual can find in the marketplace are animal products and plant products. Animal products include any foods that either are a part of an animal or are produced by an animal, such as meat, milk, assorted dairy products, and honey. Plant products are foods that originate from some sort of vegetation and include foods such as fruits, vegetables, syrup, nuts, oils, and rice. It is important for an individual to understand the difference between these two groups, as animal products often have more foodborne illnesses associated with them than do plant products; because of this, there are different methods of storing and preparing each type of food to minimize these risks. Animal products and plant products provide different nutrients that the body requires to

-24-

continue functioning normally, so a healthy individual would need to eat both animal and plant products to receive enough of the various nutrients he or she requires without the use of vitamin supplements.

Factors that might influence what foods are available

Some of the major factors that might influence what foods are available to a consumer include the region in which a consumer lives, current weather conditions and seasonal effects, and the demand for a particular type of food. Each geographical region has its own natural resources and different climate, which results in foods unique to the area being readily available. For example, certain crops that react poorly to sudden temperature drops, such as oranges, are easier to grow in areas that have relatively stable and warm climates. Weather and seasonal conditions also play a large role in whether a particular food is available, as certain foods may not be produced during some times of the year in a particular region, while other crops may die as a result of hurricanes, droughts, and other natural disasters. The demand for a particular type of food can also have a significant impact on the availability of that food. Oftentimes, if the demand for a particular type of food increases suddenly, suppliers may have difficulty in meeting that demand.

Unit pricing

Unit pricing is the practice of indicating the price of a product based on the cost per piece or unit included in that product. In other words, unit pricing is a method of determining how much an item costs per unit of measurement. For example, a 12-pack of 12-ounce cans of soda might be $2.99 and have a unit price of $0.70 per liter. Unit pricing is important because it can be extremely useful to a consumer who is attempting to compare two similar products of different sizes to determine which product is less expensive. If, for instance, an individual is trying to decide between a 12-pack of soda that costs $2.99 and has a unit price of $0.70 per liter and a six pack that retails for $1.99 and has a unit price of $0.93 per liter, he or she can easily compare unit prices and see that the 12 pack is the better buy.

Food distributors

Some of the major types of food distributors a consumer might find in the marketplace are chain supermarkets, independent grocery stores, farmers' markets, restaurants, and local farm stands. Each type of food distribution center has its own distinct advantages and disadvantages. Chain supermarkets are large stores that usually offer a large selection of foods at mid-range prices, but foods are often not as fresh and are sometimes of poorer quality than a consumer might find at a farm stand or farmers' market. Independent grocery stores and farmers markets usually have a smaller selection and are slightly more expensive than chain supermarkets, but many consumers prefer to purchase food from these sources because the food is usually locally grown and fresher. Even though restaurants are the most expensive distributors of food because the food is prepared by the restaurant for the consumer, many people appreciate the quality and variety of foods a restaurant can offer. Local farm stands frequently offer the freshest, highest-quality foods for the lowest prices, but they are open for shorter periods of time, often seasonally.

Food consumption patterns

Food consumption patterns are comprised of an analysis of the eating habits of people belonging to a particular region or area. Food consumption patterns indicate that individuals from different regions have very different diets and therefore receive more—or less—of certain nutrients than individuals from other regions. Knowing the kinds of nutrients that are common in the everyday diets of individuals native to a particular area is important, as that information allows health care professionals to understand what types of diseases and deficiencies pose a threat to the people of that region. By understanding which diseases and vitamin deficiencies the individuals of a particular area may be suffering from, resources can be allocated for treating and preventing those diseases. Monitoring food consumption patterns also allows researchers to study these patterns and determine the ingredients in certain foods that may be contributing to illnesses that are prevalent in a particular region.

Eating preferences

Just as every individual is fond of certain foods, her or she dislikes or refuses to eat other types of foods as well. In general, people will find the foods that offer them the most physiological and psychological satisfaction to be the most appealing. Most people who refuse to eat a particular food usually do so for one of three basic reasons: they dislike the taste of the food, the condition of the food or how the food was produced is unappealing to them, or they fear that the food will make them ill. Such preferences are important because they serve as one of the body's safety mechanisms to prevent individuals from eating foods that may be contaminated or foods that the individual may be allergic to. In some circumstances, however, an individual's eating preferences may need to be ignored so that the body can receive all of the nutrients it needs.

Protecting consumers from unsafe foods and keeping food affordable

A number of government regulations in the United States are intended to protect consumers from unsafe foods and help keep food affordable. Some of the most important regulations include food subsidies, price ceilings, tariffs and import quotas, quality-control inspections, and sanitation regulations. Government regulations can manage and even reduce the price of food in several ways: imposing tariffs on imported foods, limiting the amounts of particular foods that can enter the country, offering American farmers and food production facilities financial incentives, and then limiting how much those subsidized producers can charge for their goods. Ideally, these techniques help keep local food sources in business so that the United States does not have to rely too much on outside food sources. Government regulated quality-control inspections and sanitation regulations, such as the Egg Products Inspection Act, the Federal Meat Inspection Act, and the Sanitary Food Transportation Act, all have the purpose of ensuring that foods are produced, stored, and transported following certain guidelines to prevent the food from being contaminated.

Reducing the risk of foodborne illnesses

Some of the methods that can be used to reduce the risk of foodborne illnesses include thawing food appropriately to prevent the growth of bacteria, storing perishable foods in airtight containers and keeping them refrigerated or frozen, and sanitizing all cooking areas and cooking equipment. Individuals should wash their hands before and after handling raw foods, as well as wash fruits and vegetables before eating to remove any bacteria and pesticides. In addition, foods, especially meats, should be cooked at a high enough temperature for a long enough period of time to avoid the growth of bacteria that lead to foodborne illnesses. Perishable foods should be stored in temperatures of 40 degrees Fahrenheit or below to prevent the growth of bacteria, and frozen foods should be thawed in the refrigerator rather than left out to thaw at room temperature because bacteria grows most quickly at temperatures between 41 degrees and 140 degrees Fahrenheit.

Deciding what cooking equipment to purchase

Some of the factors that a consumer should consider when choosing what cooking equipment to purchase include the materials used in the construction of the cooking equipment, the heat conductivity of the materials used, the energy conservation of the cooking equipment, and how easy the equipment is to use and clean. The materials that are used in the construction of a piece of cooking equipment are important because certain materials conduct heat more effectively, retain heat more efficiently, are more durable, and are less expensive than other materials. Certain materials are also rustproof, stick-resistant, and easy to clean, do not flake, and do not react to certain foods. Both the heat conductivity and energy conservation of a piece of cooking equipment are also relevant because the greater the conductivity of the material used in the construction of the equipment and the more efficiently it can retain the heat, the faster the food will cook. Consumers should also know that some types of cooking equipment are easier to use and clean than others, which can make food preparation and clean-up faster.

Food irradiation and shelf life

Food irradiation is the process of using radioactive materials to disinfect and preserve certain types of food. Shelf life refers to how long food will last before it spoils and begins to breed bacteria. Irradiation is important for food manufacturers because it allows a facility to use varying amounts of radiation to kill any bacteria that might be growing on a particular food item, thereby reducing a consumer's risk of foodborne illness. As a result of irradiation techniques that prevent or slow the growth of bacteria, the shelf life of many foods is significantly lengthened. Studies have shown that irradiation methods are completely safe and pose no noticeable risk to individuals who eat foods that have been treated. Foods that are commonly irradiated include apples, bananas, fish, onions, poultry, potatoes, red meats, and strawberries.

Dietary Guidelines for Americans

The Dietary Guidelines for Americans is a combined publication of the United States Department of Health and Human Services and the United States Department of Agriculture that offers advice to consumers about dietary choices that promote good health and reduce the risk of certain diseases, including hypertension, anemia, and osteoporosis. The Dietary Guidelines for Americans offers advice to consumers on a variety of topics such as weight management, appropriate exercise, food safety, and examples of good sources of certain nutrients. This publication is important because it offers a detailed outline of the kinds of foods that an individual should have in their diets, so they do not need to use additional supplements and vitamins. It also informs consumers of the types of exercise that are necessary for an individual to stay healthy as well as the appropriate manner in which to handle and prepare certain foods to minimize the risk of foodborne illness.

The United States Department of Agriculture began issuing nutrition guidelines in 1894, and in 1943 the department began promoting the Basic 7 food groups. In 1956, Basic 7 was replaced with the Basic Four food groups. These were fruits and vegetables, cereals and breads, milk, and meat. Basic Four lasted until 1992, when it was replaced with the Food Pyramid, which divided food into six groups: 1) Bread, cereal, rice, pasta 2) Fruit 3) Vegetables 4) Meat, poultry, fish, dry beans, eggs, nuts 5) Milk, yogurt, cheese 6) Fats, oils, sweets. The Food Pyramid also provided recommendations for the number of daily servings from each group.

The USDA's Food Pyramid was heavily criticized for being vague and confusing, and in 2011 it was replaced with MyPlate. MyPlate is much easier to understand, as it consists of a picture of a dinner plate divided into four sections, visually illustrating how our daily diet should be distributed among the various food groups. Vegetables and grains each take up 30% of the plate, while fruits and proteins each constitute 20% of the plate. There is also a representation of a cup, marked Dairy, alongside the plate. The idea behind MyPlate is that it's much easier for people to grasp the idea that half of a meal should consist of fruits and vegetables than it is for them to understand serving sizes for all the different kinds of foods they eat on a regular basis.

Most experts consider MyPlate to be a great improvement over the Food Pyramid, but it has still come under criticism from some quarters. Many believe too much emphasis is placed on protein, and some say the dairy recommendation should be eliminated altogether. The Harvard School of Public Health created its own Healthy Eating Plate to address what it sees as shortcomings in MyPlate. Harvard's guide adds healthy plant-based oils to the mix, stresses whole grains instead of merely grains, recommends drinking water or unsweetened coffee or tea instead of milk, and adds a reminder that physical activity is important.

Resource Management

Time management

Some of the techniques used in time management include setting goals, planning the best way to complete a task, scheduling, prioritizing tasks, making sure that all necessary equipment is easily accessible, and effectively managing one's workload. A successful time management system successfully incorporates all of these techniques, with the end result of accomplishing the most tasks possible in the amount of time given.

Prioritizing activities

One of the most important techniques in time management is prioritizing so that the most important tasks are completed first and the least important tasks are left for when a person has more time available to do them. This system allows people to rank both goals and the corresponding tasks that lead to achieving those goals based on how essential they are to the individual or the organization. An individual, family, or organization can determine what activities are important by first identifying and defining which goals need to be achieved in order to continue functioning. Once this step is completed, people can then decide what tasks are the most crucial for the individual or organization to continue functioning. These tasks should be given the highest priority, while less important tasks, although they also can lead to goal accomplishment, should be considered a lower priority.

Goals and decision-making

A goal is a particular purpose that an individual or organization wants to achieve in the near or distant future. In a corporate setting, for example, a goal could be achieving a specified amount of sales in the next quarter. In a family setting, a goal might be for a teenager in the family to find a job before the end of summer.

Decision-making is the process by which an individual or group attempts to determine what would be the best managerial selection from a set of possible options and/or actions from a managerial perspective, usually for the purpose of achieving a particular goal. For instance, a couple looking for a new home may make a list of the advantages and disadvantages of living in each house they view to help them decide which house to buy.

Goal-setting

Goal-setting is important because it allows individuals and organizations to identify what objectives they seek to accomplish and then determine the best means by which to accomplish those objectives. Goal-setting typically involves establishing a particular timeframe in which a goal should be achieved. Knowing what goals he or she is striving to reach in a set amount of time helps motivate each individual involved to reach that ultimate objective. Goals also provide the individual or organization with a means of measuring the amount of effort—or lack thereof—that each individual puts into obtaining those goals. In a corporate setting, goals can also provide the organization with a way to measure its overall success, which in turn can be important in determining what future actions the organization will need to take.

Valid goal

Individuals or organizations attempting to set a goal can follow the common management mnemonic SMART (specific, measurable, achievable, relevant, and time-related) to make sure that their goal is well-defined, valid, and useful when both measuring success and motivating the organization as a whole. Established goals should be specific and well-defined, have some way of being measured accurately, be attainable, and be relevant to the tasks that need to be completed for the success of the organization. The individual or organization should also decide upon an appropriate amount of time that should be spent in achieving a goal not only to make sure that it is achieved in a timely fashion, but also to ensure that the goal can be compared to other goals in the future.

1. A manager of a local retailer that usually does somewhere between $35,000 and $60,000 a week decided that his or her store should set a goal of making $50,000 in sales a week each week for the month of November.

This example demonstrates a completely valid goal, as the goal is well-defined and quantifiable. It can be measured by examining the amount of sales the store has done each week. In addition, the goal is relevant to the store's ability to make a profit within a set amount of time, as the goal of $50,000 is achievable because it falls within the store's normal sales range.

2. The mother of a child who is having difficulty in school has decided that her son needs to improve his grades.

While the goal of improving the child's grades may be achievable and relevant to the success of the child, it is not well-defined enough to be considered a valid, effective goal. Although the goal could be measured, no criteria are established as to what would be satisfactory improvement in the boy's grades. Furthermore, the mother has not established a timeframe in which her son is expected to reach the goal.

Working effectively toward achieving any given goal

Both internal and external factors can have an effect on whether an individual or organization will be able to achieve a particular goal. However, the most important thing for an individual or organization to keep in mind, regardless of the situation, is that everyone involved in the goal-attaining process should remain focused on the goal and the appropriate ways by which to achieve that goal. This means that if a goal is important to the success of the individual or the organization as a whole, people must be committed to giving their best efforts to achieve that particular goal. Any less important or irrelevant goals should not be allowed to distract the individual or the organization from the primary goal; any secondary goals should ultimately be put aside until the primary goal is achieved. From a managerial standpoint, it is important that people are regularly encouraged to recognize that the goal is achievable so that no one gives up before the goal is actually reached.

Decision-making process

The decision-making process is important because understanding the process can aid in the discovery of a future rational and reasonable course of action when an individual or organization is presented with a decision that must be made. Each individual has a unique perspective and therefore a different way of reaching a particular decision; through a combination of intuition, knowledge, and an understanding of how the decision-making process works, a decision that is best suited for the goals of a particular individual or group can be made. Effective, knowledgeable decision making consists of identifying the decision that needs to be made, recognizing the benefits of each choice related to that decision, analyzing the potential drawbacks of making each choice related to that decision, and, finally, actually making a choice. By understanding what specifically needs to be identified at each stage of the decision-making process, an individual or organization will be able to make a more informed decision that will be more likely to lead to the achievement of a particular goal.

An individual who is in the process of making a well-informed decision will often gather as much information as possible from as many reliable sources as possible, list the advantages and disadvantages of each choice, and then compare each choice with the others. In an employment or business situation where finances are involved, an individual may use a mathematical approach and calculate exactly how much money each job choice or each potential new product could offer, as well as how much a poor decision might cost if something goes wrong. A mathematical approach can be an extremely solid strategy when one is attempting to determine what choice might be the most appropriate. Unfortunately, many individuals do not make well-informed decisions because they oftentimes employ faulty methods of decision making. In such instances, they may rely too heavily on the opinions of their peers, gather information from such unreliable sources as erroneous web sites, or even leave the decision to random chance by flipping a coin.

Some of the most common pitfalls that should be avoided when attempting to make a well-informed decision are entering the decision-making process with a preconceived notion that the individual is unwilling to abandon, allowing peer pressure to influence a decision, and overgeneralizing. Entering the decision-making process with a prejudice either for or against a particular idea, source of information, or choice will often lead to the selection of an option that is not the best or most logical choice available. While outside sources should be used to gather information about the decision that needs to be made, no single source should be allowed to pressure the individuals involved in making the decision into making a particular choice. Furthermore, the overuse of generalizations, stereotypes, and attempts to attribute effects to causes that may not have any logical link will often lead to a decision being made that may not be the best course of action.

Some of the most common decision-making strategies that a business or other organization might use when making a decision include the Pareto analysis system, a cost/benefit analysis strategy, a force field analysis strategy, a grid analysis strategy, and a scenario analysis strategy. Because each strategy has its own advantages and disadvantages, businesses and other types of organizations will usually select the system or systems that best support the kind of decision they are attempting to make. For example, a Pareto analysis system can be useful when an organization is attempting to handle a group of related problems that are discovered to be responsible for most of the difficulties that the organization is experiencing. However, a Pareto analysis system will not work as well, if at all, in situations where a large number of problems are caused by completely unrelated factors.

Pareto analysis system

Basically, the Pareto analysis system is a decision-making model which assumes that approximately 80% of the benefits that an organization receives from a particular task are the result of 20% of the effort that the various individuals within the organization put into the task. It also assumes that 80% of the problems that the organization faces are produced by approximately 20% of the factors that may be causing them. The first step necessary in using the Pareto analysis system is to list all of the problems that need to be addressed and/or the choices that are available. Next, each of those problems or choices should be grouped so that the choices offering similar benefits and/or the factors leading to larger related problems are grouped together. Each group is then given a score based on how much that particular group affects the overall organization.

Cost/benefit analysis strategy

Cost/benefit analysis is a decision-making strategy that examines the total estimated cost of each option that is available alongside the total estimated benefit of each option available and then compares the cost with the benefit to determine if the benefits of the option outweigh their cost. Usually, a cost/benefit analysis refers to the financial cost and benefit of a particular decision, but it can actually be used in any situation in which resources are used. For example, if a corporation has two clothing materials, A and B, that both cost the same but material B can be used more efficiently, the cost/benefit analysis would show that material B is the best choice because it allows for the production of the most clothing using the least amount of material. While cost/benefit analysis can be useful when deciding which option will have the greatest benefit, this method also relies heavily on estimation, which makes it not as accurate as other methods of analysis.

Force field analysis strategy

Force field analysis is a decision-making strategy that examines all of the factors that affect a particular situation and identifies those factors as either aiding the organization in achieving a goal or ultimately causing the organization to fall short of reaching its specified goal. Basically, force field analysis is the process of identifying and listing which factors involved with each option help the organization and which ones hurt the organization. The first step of the force field analysis strategy is to make a list of all of the factors involved with a particular option and then identify them as either aiding the organization in moving towards a particular goal or hindering the organization's movement towards that goal. Each factor is then given a rating on a scale of 1 to 5, with 1 being the weakest and 5 being the strongest. If the forces that hinder the organization are have higher numbers, indicating that they are stronger overall, the option is probably not a sensible or realistic choice; however, if the forces that aid the organization have higher numbers, then the option may prove beneficial.

Grid analysis strategy

Grid analysis is a decision-making strategy that takes all of the factors involved with each option, rates each factor, and then gives each factor a weight based on its importance to the overall decision. For example, if the owner of a clothing factory had three materials and was attempting to decide which material would provide the most profit, he or she might consider each material's cost, how much material is wasted during the manufacturing process, and how difficult each material is to use. The owner would then rate the materials using a set scale—from 0 to 5, for example, with 0 being the most expensive or most wasteful and 5 being the least expensive or least wasteful—and rate the cost, waste, and difficulty of each material's use. By using a similar scale, the owner would then assign the factors of each option a weight based on the effect each factor has on the company's overall profit. Finally, the owner would determine a weighted score by multiplying the weight by the rating that each factor received. The material with the highest total score would be the best option.

Scenario analysis strategy

The scenario analysis strategy is a decision-making method whereby individuals or organizations use their experience, knowledge, and intuition to predict what kind of situations may arise from each option if that particular option were chosen. In other words, decision-makers employing the scenario analysis strategy attempt to determine all of the possible outcomes of a particular choice and what effect each outcome might have on the organization or individual as a whole if that choice were made. In some instances, especially in a business setting, each of these potential outcomes might be assigned a score based on how likely it is that each scenario will actually occur. However, anticipating every possible outcome that might occur and accurately predicting what events are most likely to occur in the future can be impossible.

Resources

A resource is anything that can be used to aid either in the daily functioning of an individual or organization or in the achievement of a particular goal. The four primary types of resources are land and natural resources, labor resources, capital and capital goods, and information resources. Land and natural resources consist of anything that comes from the environment, such as water, oil, soil, timber, and the land itself. Labor resources are comprised of the actual effort that various people involved in an organization put into a project, leading to the completion of that project. Capital and capital goods consist of any financial and human-made resources, including money, tools, equipment, buildings, and houses. Information resources are any resources that allow an individual or organization to find, compile, and put to use knowledge that might help in achieving a particular goal.

An individual or organization that is assessing whether enough resources are available for a particular project might begin by determining exactly what the project consists of and researching how much the project will cost in both time and money. After the individual or organization has developed a basic outline of what the project needs, an inventory of what resources are readily available should be conducted. This inventory would include noting such resources as how much money has been allocated for the project, how many people are available to work on the project, what kind of equipment is available to complete the project, and whether workers have sufficient information regarding the project to complete it. If the individual or organization determines that the resources necessary to complete the project are not available, then the project is not realistic.

A family that is attempting to determine the status of its financial resources should first collect all of the financial records from each source of income that it has. The family should then list all of its assets, including the amount of cash the family has on hand, along with the amount of cash it could get by selling any stocks, bonds, mutual funds, and property that it owns. After adding up all of its on-hand assets and potential assets, the family should then list all of its loans, unpaid bills, balances due, and financial obligations and add the numbers together to get the family's total amount of liability. By subtracting its estimated total liability from its estimated total assets, the family will get a good estimation of its financial standing in terms of its net worth.

Change management

Change management is the process by which an organization attempts to modify a particular aspect of how it operates with as little harm to the organization as possible. In most cases, an organization makes these operational changes either to adapt to changes in societal or economic demands or to improve the organization's overall operations. Although everything undergoes change at some point, many individuals have difficulty adapting to social, economic, or other changes despite how important adapting to these changes might be. Organizations that want to continue functioning must respond to changes by using change management techniques that do not place too much unnecessary stress upon the members of the organization.

The three main strategies an organization can use when making changes in its overall functions are the empirical-rational strategy, the normative-reeducative strategy, and the power-coercive strategy. Each strategy has its own advantages and disadvantages, and which strategy an organization chooses is usually based on how much the organization needs to change and what resources are available to relieve problems that may be caused by particular changes. Which strategy an organization uses may also be based heavily on how much time is available to make the changes and how many members of the organization will resist the changes.

Empirical-rational strategy

The empirical-rational strategy of managing change assumes that people are ultimately interested in their own well being and will more quickly accept changes if they believe that those changes offer them some sort of benefit. In other words, the empirical-rational strategy of managing change relies on either offering an incentive to the members of the organization who take part in a change or convincing the members of the organization that the change will benefit them in some way. For example, if a company's board of directors realized that the company's competitors had employees who were performing more effectively because they had more education, the board might decide to use an empirical-rational strategy to encourage its employees to go back to school. By offering to pay for additional schooling and/or offering promotions, raises, or other incentives, the board of directors could encourage some of their employees to seek further education and, as a result, be better trained for their professional lives.

Normative-reeducative strategy

The normative-reeducative strategy of managing change revolves around the idea that peer pressure can bring about the changes that an organization needs. Basically, this strategy assumes that people rely heavily on social interaction and therefore will normally behave according to the expectations of society. Using this assumption, an organization can institute new changes by gradually redefining aspects of the organization's structure and purpose, and each individual will then begin to accept the changes as part of the social norm. For example, if the board of directors of a retail chain realizes that customer service is becoming a more important marketing point than the price of goods, the directors may institute a normative-reeducative strategy. The company would then begin emphasizing desirable customer-service behaviors by placing posters in the break room that affirm the importance of customer service, holding meetings and performance reviews that address appropriate ways to treat customers, and training new employees in good customer service tactics.

Power-coercive strategy

The power-coercive strategy of managing change assumes that people will listen to authority figures and do as they are told. This strategy works by preventing the members of the organization from choosing any option other than the path that the manager wants them to follow, mainly because no other acceptable options are available to them. If an individual still refuses to accept the changes that the organization has implemented, the organization might punish the individual for not complying. In a family situation, if a child is doing poorly in school because he is spending too much time watching television, the child's mother might simply turn off the TV and tell her child to do his homework. If the child turns the television back on, his mother might send him to his room and ground him for a week as punishment for disobeying.

Advantages and disadvantages of each of the three main types of strategies used in managing changes within an organization

While the empirical-rational strategy is very effective when an organization has enough available resources to offer the incentives necessary to make changes more acceptable to employees, it is much less successful if the organization does not offer substantial enough incentives. The changes must have an obvious benefit to the individuals who need to implement them. The normative-reeducative strategy is useful when the managers and workers of an organization have a strong relationship and have time available to implement the changes; however, this strategy is much less effective when relations between management and staff are strained or when employees feel rushed or obligated to execute the changes. The power-coercive strategy is particularly useful in situations where time is limited and the threat to the organization or individual is more crucial; however, this method can often promote unrest among members of the organization, especially in organizations that have traditionally allowed more individual freedoms.

Consumer rights

Consumer rights consist of a series of protections, usually guaranteed by law, that seek to prevent individuals from being taken advantage of in the marketplace. In the United States, a large number of state and federal laws establish the rights of consumers, rights that are enforced by the consumer affairs departments of each state, the Federal Trade Commission, and the U.S. Justice Department. Some examples of federal acts that have guaranteed certain rights to consumers are the Equal Credit Opportunity Act, the Fair Housing Act, the Fair Credit Reporting Act, the Fair Debt Collection Practices Act, and the Truth in Lending Act. All

- 35 -

of these federal acts and state laws are important because they help prevent consumers from wasting their finances by spending them on products or services that have been sold to them under unethical business practices. Some of these acts also protect the consumer from being discriminated against by businesses or individuals that harbor prejudices against certain consumers.

Time management

Time management is the process of using skills, tools, principles, and practices together in order to most efficiently use the time that an individual or group of individuals has available. The efficiency goal of time management is similar to that of work simplification; however, time management itself does not actually make work easier. Instead, time management involves finding the most proficient way to complete a task at hand in the amount of time given. Time management is extremely important in both business and personal settings, as people often do not have enough time available to complete every single task they face. Planning how to complete the greatest number of tasks possible in the amount of time available allows people to get more value out of their time and efforts.

Using different types of resources

Land resources can be used as locations for homes and businesses or as sites for other natural resources located on a piece of land, such as oil, minerals, soil that can be used for planting, and water for drinking and fishing. Examples of people who can be considered labor resources are marketers who determine the best way to sell a product, salespeople who sell the product to the consumer, factory workers who assemble that product, and anyone else who aids in achieving the end goal of those dealing with the product. Capital refers specifically to money, but capital goods include the machinery that turns raw goods into a finished product in a factory. Information resources may be books or online sites that can be used to learn how to construct a better product or how to better manage a particular organization. All of these resources can be used in a variety of ways, and most projects require a combination of different types of resources.

Importance of non-financial resources to a family during difficult economic times

Non-financial resources, or resources that are not cash or cannot be sold outright and turned into cash, can be extremely useful to a family that is experiencing financial problems. Non-financial resources can often be used to produce income or reduce costs that the family is experiencing. For example, a family that may not want to sell its house can rent out a room to make additional money. A family member who is a seamstress could lower the family's costs by mending everyone's clothing instead of throwing it away and buying new garments. A carpenter in the family could make necessary repairs to the family home, eliminating the cost of paying anyone else for labor. Any skill that a family member possesses can help cut the family's costs, and any service the family can offer to people outside the home can serve as a way of gathering additional income.

Identifying and defining the goals and values before making a decision

Identifying and defining the goals that a family or other organization needs to meet and the moral values that the family or organization wants to uphold can be extremely important prior to any decision because doing so offers a guide as to what options are unacceptable

- 36 -

before an incorrect choice is made. By setting well-defined goals to achieve in the future, a family or organization can choose the options that appear to move it closer to the achievement of those goals. Defining the family's or organization's moral values is also important, because doing so aids in eliminating choices that might be directly opposed to what the family or organization considers correct and ethical.

Basic rights that consumer laws protect

The overall purpose of any consumer law is to uphold the three basic rights of the consumer: the right to safety, the right to be informed, and the right to be treated fairly. Federal and state laws are usually designed to protect one or more of these basic rights and may include protections against products that are dangerous, protections against deceptive business tactics or hidden costs associated with a transaction, and protections against certain types of discrimination within the marketplace. Ultimately, state and federal laws are designed to hold businesses accountable for the manner in which they conduct business.

Equal Credit Opportunity Act and the Fair Housing Act

The Equal Credit Opportunity Act is a federal act prohibiting any organization that issues credit to consumers from denying credit to a consumer on the basis of race, gender, age, marital status, religion, national origin, or skin color. The act also prohibits any organization from denying a consumer credit if he or she is receiving federal aid or has previously used another of their rights granted to them by federal law so long as the consumer used that right without malicious intent. If a consumer is denied credit, the organization issuing the denial is required by law to send the denial notification in writing, and the consumer has 60 days to request that the organization send the reason for the denial in writing as well. The Fair Housing Act is a similar anti-discrimination act that prevents a seller or organization offering financing for a home from denying to sell, rent, or finance a residence on the basis of race, color, gender, religion, family status, national origin, or handicap.

Fair Credit Reporting Act

The Fair Credit Reporting Act states that consumer reporting agencies collecting and distributing information about consumers for credit related purposes are required to follow certain guidelines concerning how they maintain and distribute the information they collect. This act requires consumer reporting agencies to follow a series of procedures established by law to verify and correct mistakes on a consumer's credit record if a consumer makes a dispute. Agencies must also keep records confidential and release them only to businesses that have a legitimate need for those records. This act also sets limits as to how long certain negative information can be kept on record. If a negative piece of information is removed through a dispute, that information cannot be added back onto a consumer's record without notifying the consumer in writing within 5 days. This act was later amended by the Fair and Accurate Credit Transactions Act to allow consumers the right to receive one free copy of their credit report from the three major credit reporting agencies each year.

Fair Debt Collection Practices Act

The Fair Debt Collection Practices Act requires third party debt collectors, businesses that collect debts due to other individuals or businesses, to refrain from using abusive or

- 37 -

deceptive practices in collecting those debts. This act prohibits such actions as calling consumers at times other than in between 8:00 a.m. and 9:00 p.m. local time and contacting consumers in any manner other than filing a lawsuit if the consumer has given written notice not to contact him or her regarding the debt. This act also prohibits the collection agency from such practices as adding extra fees and charges to the original balance unless allowed by law, threatening consumers with arrest or legal action that is not permissible by law, or reporting false information on a consumer's credit report. This act also requires third party debt collectors to identify themselves as a debt collector to the consumer during every communication and to provide verification of the original debt upon request.

Truth in Lending Act

The Truth in Lending Act requires any organization issuing credit to a consumer to disclose the full terms of the lending arrangement and all costs associated with entering into that arrangement. This means that when a consumer applies for a loan, a credit card, or any other type of credit, the organization must provide the consumer with information about finance charges, the annual percentage rate for the loan, and any additional fees associated with the loan arrangement. In addition to establishing a procedure for the fair and timely handling of billing disputes related to credit transactions, this act also limits the amount of money that a consumer can be held liable for if his or her credit card is lost or stolen.

Responsible consumer

Even though state and federal laws exist to protect consumers from unethical business practices, preventing every type of unscrupulous tactic from being used is not always possible. As a result, consumers should be knowledgeable about their rights to avoid being scammed. Many businesses adhere to legal standards and do not employ tactics that are illegal or unethical. However, some businesses choose to do what is profitable instead of what is ethical. Finding loopholes in regulations allows businesses to make claims about their products that may not necessarily be true without being held legally accountable for those claims. Unethical business operations have also been known to find ways to charge consumers additional fees that are legally questionable. In spite of the number of laws designed to protect them, consumers must be diligent about protecting their own interests when making transactions in the marketplace.

Caveat emptor

The Latin phrase "caveat emptor" literally means "let the buyer beware." This expression suggests that a buyer needs to be aware of products or services that may be defective or not as useful as the buyer had anticipated. Some states have laws that create implied warranties regarding certain types of products and allow a consumer the right to return a product that is defective. However, even implied warranties do not protect the consumer from some kinds of defects and protect the consumer only from defects that show up before a certain period of time has passed. If the product or service is not what the consumer thought it was and the seller made no deliberate attempt to defraud the consumer, the seller is typically under no legal obligation to take the product back or refund the consumer's money.

Before making any purchase that requires a financial investment, a consumer should gather as much information as possible about the product or service he or she plans to buy. By finding out what other consumers have said about a particular product and discovering exactly what the product is and is not capable of doing, a consumer can avoid purchasing a product that is defective or less useful than he or she originally thought. A consumer can also research what kinds of problems other consumers have had with the product, as well as compare the quality and uses of similar products to determine if another product would be a better match for the needs of the consumer. Because the seller of a product is not under any obligation to inform a consumer about how the product compares in price, quality, and usefulness to other products, it is the consumer's responsibility to know exactly what he or she is getting when making a purchase.

Wants and needs

A want is anything that a person desires, as opposed to a need, which is anything that a person requires to continue functioning. A plasma television, for example, is a want because it is not necessary to an individual's continued survival. An example of needs would be food and water, both of which are things an individual requires to survive. Because people are inherently different, wants or desires vary from person to person. Typically, a person has more desires than his or her resources can fulfill. Needs, however, are universal because they are everyone's basic necessities and must be met for the continued existence of an individual.

Decision process that a consumer usually goes through to make a purchase

The first step of the decision process for any consumer planning to make a purchase is recognizing that he or she has a need or a want that to fulfill. After the want or need has been identified, the consumer typically gathers information about products or services that will fulfill that need or want by searching online, examining magazines and advertisements, or talking with other people. The consumer will then evaluate the various product or service choices available in order to determine which option will best fulfill that need or want. Once the consumer's options have been evaluated, he or she will decide which product or service is most suitable and make the purchase. After the purchase is complete, the consumer will be able to decide whether or not that product or service really satisfied the initial want or need that initiated the decision process.

Marketing

Marketing is the process of informing as many consumers as possible of the existence of a particular product or service and the benefits of that product or service with the intent of influencing a consumer's purchasing decisions. In other words, marketing is a combination of tactics that includes many different forms of advertising that individuals, businesses, and other organizations use to convince consumers to purchase their products. Marketing is important because it allows businesses to play a large role in what consumers actually purchase. Consumers may have the final say in what products or services they decide to use, but marketing can make certain products seem more appealing, more useful, and of a higher quality than a consumer would normally believe them to be. Marketing can also be useful to consumers by informing them about various useful products within the marketplace; however, consumers should be wary of claims and advertisements made by marketers that may make products seem better than they really are.

Marketing can influence almost every stage of the consumer's purchase decision process, but it has the greatest direct effect on the first three stages of the process. The first stage of the process can be triggered by an advertisement marketing a certain product that the consumer may not normally consider to be necessary. By creating the idea or image that a product or service is something necessary to the consumer, a business can make something the consumer wants appear to be something the consumer needs. Marketing can also directly influence the second and third stages of the decision making process by making a product appear better or more useful than competing products, even though this may not necessarily be true. The marketing process can even indirectly influence the fourth stage of the process; consumers actually purchase the product because they have the preconceived notion that a certain product is better than other similar products as a result of the advertisements that they have seen.

State of the economy

The economy plays an important role in how careful consumers are when using their resources and what they perceive as needs as opposed to what they perceive as wants. When the economy is doing well, unemployment figures are low, which means that people can easily attain their basic necessities. As a result, consumers will are typically more willing to spend their financial resources. Consumers will also be more willing to spend their resources on products and services that are not necessary to their survival, but are instead products and services that consumers enjoy having and believe increase their quality of life. On the other hand, when the economy is in a slump, consumers are much more likely to cut back on their spending because they perceive a significantly higher risk of being unable to acquire basic necessities due to a lack of financial resources.

Environmental concerns

The condition of the natural environment can affect the purchasing decisions of a consumer in two major ways. First, most consumers, due to their own personal values or the values of society, are at least somewhat concerned with the state of the environment around them and will seek ways to prevent unnecessary waste. However, hardly anyone will always purchase the most environmentally-friendly products and conserve every possible resource at all times, but consumers will often choose to purchase products that are recycled or less wasteful when they are available and are not significantly more expensive. The second major way that the environment can affect the purchasing decisions of a consumer involves a consumer's decision to conserve a particular resource because that resource has become more expensive due to a shortage. For example, if an area experiences a gas shortage, the prices of gas will rise significantly, and many consumers will conserve gas to avoid paying higher prices.

The primary way that consumers can help protect the environment is by conserving natural resources and finding ways to reduce pollution and waste. Some of the best ways to conserve natural resources include reducing the amount of resources that a household uses, finding ways to use resources more efficiently, and reusing resources rather than simply discarding them. For example, a household can reduce the amount of resources it consumes by turning off the lights and heat in an unused room or by insulating outside walls to reduce the amount of heat that is lost in a room. A household can also participate in area recycling programs or find new uses for items, such as using a cardboard box that a product came in to store other household items.

Environmental economics

Environmental economics is the study of the effects that businesses and consumers have on the overall financial and natural environment when operating within set limits. In other words, environmental economics studies how much pollution actually costs based on the costs or savings associated with pollution and the amount of environmental resources lost due to that pollution. Environmental economics is important to businesses and consumers because it can influence what products are available and what processes can be used in manufacturing those products. Based on environmental economists' recommendations, laws and regulations are made to reduce the amount of damage done to financial and natural environments due to the inefficient or irresponsible use of natural resources. Even though these laws ultimately exist to prevent the waste of natural resources, these regulations can result in the elimination of some products from the marketplace, as well as significant cost increases to the end consumer as businesses incur additional costs in meeting those regulations.

Private and government agencies that can provide resources to consumers

A number of agencies can provide resources that help inform consumers about the advantages, disadvantages, and even the scams related to certain products and services. Some of the government agencies that are most useful to consumers are the Federal Citizen Information Center, the Consumer Product Safety Commission, the National Fraud Information Center, and the Federal Trade Commission. All of these agencies have extensive information online, as well as available print publications, about many of the most common products on the market. Probably the most well known and useful private agencies to consumers are Consumer's Research, a non-profit agency that publishes the magazine *Consumer Reports*, and the Better Business Bureau, which is a private organization made up of businesses that sets certain standards which its members are expected to follow.

Housing

The primary purpose for any type of housing is to act as a form of shelter. Shelter in this context refers to protecting people from harsh weather such as rain, snow, extreme heat, extreme cold, harsh winds, extensive exposure to UV radiation, or any other conditions that might prove unpleasant or harmful. Housing can also provide security by making it more difficult for harmful things, such as animals, insects, unscrupulous individuals, and other threats, to reach people and their belongings. In some cases, housing can also serve as a location for individuals to conduct business in and work from. A house itself can even act as a symbol of the wealth and status of its owners.

The two major types of residential housing are houses and apartments. A house is an entire building with the primary purpose of providing shelter for the individual or family that resides in it. An apartment is a section of a building that has been split into units, and the primary purpose of each unit is to provide shelter for the individual or family that lives in that unit. The major difference between and house and an apartment is that a building is considered a house if the whole building belongs to one individual, family, or several families that share the entire building or at least most of the building. On the other hand, a building is considered to be an apartment building or a complex if it contains separate sections or units that each allow individuals or families to live on their own without sharing a large portion of the building.

The three major types of houses found in the United States are single-family houses, townhouses, and semi-detached houses. A single-family house is any building used for residential use that is separate from any other buildings. Townhouses are a series of buildings where all of the houses share both of their side walls with the buildings on each side, with the exception of the houses at the ends of the row, which only share one wall. Semi-detached houses are two residential buildings that share only a single wall and have empty space on their other side. These three major types of houses are typically determined by how much space is available around the building. A single-family home has space available on all sides, a semi-detached house has space clear in front, behind, and on one side of the house, and townhouses, with the exception of the townhouses on the end of the row, have space only in front and behind the house.

Security

Security can be extremely important for an individual or group that is wealthy, well known, or at high risk of being victimized by thieves or other criminals. A home can provide a wide range of protective measures to help keep people and their belongings safe, including locks on doors and windows, burglar alarms, fire alarms, and carbon monoxide detectors to warn residents of potentially deadly threats. Some homes, especially homes that are located in high-risk areas, might contain a large number of personal assets. Those residences that house individuals who are at high risk due to their social status, political rank, or amount of personal assets, may also have additional security measures in place. These measures include security features such as strong deadbolts locks, security cameras, gates, and checkpoints.

Running a business from home

A number of advantages are associated with running a business from home. Probably the most important advantage of running a home-based business is the fact that individuals or groups can usually significantly reduce their overhead costs as a result of using a single building for both business and living purposes. Overhead costs that can be reduced include expenses related to transportation, business clothing, office furnishings, maintenance, mortgage or rent, taxes, and other similar expenses. Some of the other major advantages of running a home based business are that the individual has a more flexible schedule, has the ability to put most of the time that would be spent commuting to better use, and the individual is readily available to fulfill their domestic responsibilities as well.

For an individual to be able to work successfully and efficiently in any environment, he or she needs a private place to work that is relatively free from distractions. Regardless of what type of business an individual is attempting to run, he or she will also require time to accomplish the work that needs to be done, as well as the necessary equipment to perform that work. Equipment an individual may require for his or her home business includes a computer, printer, fax machine, telephone, and computer programs appropriate to the type of work to be performed. It is also important that an individual is able to find the storage space necessary for any equipment that the business will need to function appropriately.

The single largest problem that home business owners face is the conflict that arises between the needs of the family and the needs of the business. Every business has its own distinct needs, and those needs can be difficult to achieve in a home setting because a conflict can arise between the space, time, and equipment that the family needs and the space, time, and equipment that the business needs. For example, a child or other family member may need the business space or equipment, such as a computer, to complete his or her homework at the same time that the business owner is using the space and equipment for conducting business. On the other hand, the children of the family may not need to use the computer, but instead need the business owner to step into a parental role and feed them or help them with their homework, which distracts the business owner from the tasks he or she needs to complete for work purposes. Any equipment purchased specifically for the business will also require space that the family might have already had dedicated for another purpose in the household.

Status symbol

The major reason that a home can act as a status symbol for an individual or family that lives in it is because of the financial investment necessary to own a home. Regardless of the type of home that someone lives in, purchasing or leasing a home is usually the single largest expense that anyone will take on during his or her life. As a result, the home of an individual or family can act as an indication of the overall wealth that a person or family possesses. This means that the larger and more luxurious a house is, the greater the amount of wealth a person must have had in order to acquire that home. Since wealth is commonly associated with the status of an individual, the type of home that an individual or family lives in acts indicates their social status as well.

Apartments

The most common types of apartments found in the United States are single or multi-bedroom apartments and studio apartments. Single or multi-bedroom apartments are units that have one or more bedrooms that are separated from the rest of the unit. Studio apartments are units that have one large room that makes up the entire unit and performs the functions of a bedroom, living room, dining room, kitchen, and any other rooms that the unit's tenants require. Studio apartments and single or multi-bedroom apartments are usually rented, but it is becoming more and more common for apartments to be sold to consumers as condominiums or cooperatives. Regardless of whether an apartment is rented or purchased, studio apartments are almost always less expensive than multi-bedroom apartments; the price of an apartment increases significantly with each extra separate bedroom attached to the unit.

Condominium and cooperative

A condominium, also known as a condo, is a type of apartment ownership where an individual has purchased complete ownership of a single unit but has shared ownership of certain common areas and common expenses associated with the building. This means that the individual living in the condo owns the unit and is responsible for all of the expenses associated with that unit, but shares the rest of the building and the expenses associated with the remainder of the building. A cooperative, also known as a co-op, is a type of apartment where an individual owns shares in a corporation, and that corporation owns the entire building. An individual who owns the shares has the right to live in a particular unit within the building as long as he or she follows certain guidelines set by the corporation.

The major difference between a condominium and a cooperative is that a condo owner actually owns the unit and shares ownership of the building, while a co-op owner does not actually own the unit or the building, but rather owns part of a corporation and that corporation owns the building. By paying condo fees and discussing problems with a condo association, the owner of a condo directly shares the decisions and expenses related to the upkeep of the building. A co-op owner, on the other hand, is not directly responsible for the expenses and problems of the building as the corporation that owns the building handles these expenses and problems using the funds they gather from the rent or subscription fees paid by the co-op owners.

Renting and purchasing housing

The two most common methods that an individual or family might use to pay for their housing are renting, also known as leasing, and purchasing a house through a mortgage or loan. When an individual does not actually own a house or apartment where he or she resides, but rather pays a monthly fee for the use of that house or apartment, that is renting. People who rent a place to live will never own the property no matter how long they live there and how much rent they pay. In contrast, an individual who takes out a mortgage on a particular type of housing actually purchases that house or apartment using the money acquired from a loan.

The two major advantages of renting housing rather than purchasing housing are that renting is usually less expensive in terms of monthly payments and the individual or family does not have to be concerned with costs associated with maintaining the building. A renter or lessee does not actually own the building and has to pay only whatever fee the building's owner has set for that particular unit, regardless of any work that the rest of the building may require. For example, if a building's plumbing needs work, any cost that is associated with repairing the plumbing is the responsibility of the building's owner and not the responsibility of the apartment's tenant. The major disadvantage of renting is that the individual does not gain any long-term financial advantage from paying rent because each rent payment is not being applied toward the purchase of the property.

The major advantage of purchasing housing rather than renting is that an individual or family actually owns the property and can sell that property or rent it to someone else at a later time. Each monthly payment is applied to paying off the loan that was used to purchase the property, and the owner can decide to sell that property at any point and keep any money that is leftover after paying the bank back. An individual who is renting can leave his or her apartment at any time but will receive no benefit from the money he or she paid while living there. The two major disadvantages of purchasing a home are that the monthly payments are usually higher than what an individual renting a home pays and the individual or family is responsible for all of the expenses associated with maintaining the home.

An individual who is attempting to decide whether to rent or purchase a particular type of housing should base the decision on his or her income. This can be done by estimating how much buying a piece of property will cost the individual per month, how much renting will cost the individual per month, and the individual's monthly income. If the individual has the money available to put a reasonable down payment on a piece of property that he or she is interested in and has the income to make the monthly mortgage payments on the property without a problem, buying is usually the better option. This is because purchasing a piece of property, unlike renting, is an investment that can be sold, usually with some degree of financial return for the original property owner. On the other hand, if an individual cannot afford to make a reasonable down payment and the monthly mortgage payments are more than the he or she can comfortably afford, renting is a better option.

An individual or family that is considering what building to rent or purchase should first determine how much they can afford to spend on housing. Purchasing or even renting housing is always a major investment, and the individual or family needs to make sure that they have the funds available to make the required payments. Next, the individual or family should determine what attributes of the house or apartment are important to them, such as the location of the building, how big the building should be, how much storage space the building has, and how much yard space it includes. Once the individual or family has made a list of all of the things that should be ideal features of their house or apartment, they can then begin looking for houses or apartments that are within their price range and best suit their needs.

Area surrounding a house or apartment

Some of the most important factors regarding the surrounding area of a house or apartment that an individual should consider include the current state of the neighborhood, how accessible the property is, and the quality of local schools and recreational facilities. The current state of the neighborhood refers to factors such as the overall appearance of the neighborhood, the traffic and noise level, the number of children living in the area, parking, zoning or other regulations and restrictions, and the level of police, fire, and community involvement in the neighborhood. The accessibility of a piece of property refers to its location and how close it is to stores, public transportation, major roads and highways, and a resident's place of employment. For active individuals and families with children, quality local schools and recreational facilities are important. Considerations include how close the house or apartment is to these facilities, how well maintained these facilities are, and the reputations of these facilities.

Interior design

Interior design is the process of planning the best way possible to construct a room, a series of rooms, or an entire house. The primary purpose of interior design is to make each room both as functional and as appealing as possible. Interior designers usually consider seven basic elements of design when deciding how to make a particular room appealing: color, texture, pattern, line, shape, form, and mass. Once the interior designer knows the purpose and functional requirements of a room, he or she can then create a floor plan of how the room or rooms will fit into the rest of the house and of how the room itself will be organized to fulfill its intended purpose.

Floor plan

Some of the factors that an individual should consider when designing a floor plan include what size the room or rooms should be, what furniture needs to go in each room, how often each room will be used, and the traffic patterns of the room. The individual should also consider how many electrical outlets the room requires, how much lighting is necessary for the room, and whether the room has any special requirements to fulfill the purpose of the room. For example, a photographer who is planning to add on a darkroom to his house would need a room that is located away from outside walls and windows, lets in virtually no light, has access to a number of electrical outlets and countertops for developing equipment, and has sinks for rinsing film. A well-designed floor plan is important because it allows an individual to eliminate problems such as not enough storage space, not enough room for furniture and equipment, not enough light, and not enough access to power outlets.

Traffic patterns

An individual who is analyzing the traffic patterns of a room should consider the purpose of the room, the location of the room in relation to other rooms, the number of people that will be using the room, and the ease of movement in the room. The traffic patterns of a room refer to how many people are moving into, through, and around that room and how easy it is for them to make those movements. For example, a room that is near the center of a house and connects two rooms on different sides should have a clear, straight path entering and exiting each connecting room. This means that people walking through the room should be able to walk straight through without having to walk around couches, tables, chairs, or other furniture that is blocking their path. A room with a well-planned traffic pattern will allow people to access every part of the room without climbing over or walking around furniture.

Family and Consumer Sciences Programs and Careers

Health care

A consumer who is in need of health care services might take into account the number of complaints and the types of complaints a facility or specific doctor has received and consequently examine the qualifications of the doctors who practice in that facility. These factors are important to a consumer for any health care decision ranging from choosing a physician for a simple examination to choosing a surgeon for a complex surgery because they give the consumer a basic idea of the overall quality and reliability of the doctor and medical facility. By determining the number of complaints and the types of complaints that have been filed against a doctor or facility, a consumer can get an idea of what kinds of mistakes and how many of those mistakes the facility or doctor has made. Experience can also be a key factor in how reliable a particular doctor is and can greatly affect the quality of his or her care, as more experienced doctors are usually better capable of providing more effective care.

Unfortunately, determining the exact number of complaints a physician or facility has had filed against them is difficult because no federal law exists that requires physicians or facilities to disclose or even report information regarding complaints. However, the United States Department of Health and Services does keep track of reported complaints and is a good source of information for a consumer who is attempting to gather information about a specific doctor or medical facility. Despite the lack of federal laws, many states have laws that do require medical facilities to report the number of complaints and the nature of those complaints filed against the facility or doctors employed by the facility. In many of these states, the facility may not be obligated to disclose the information directly to patients, but a consumer can oftentimes access a state database containing the information online.

Child care services

A consumer should consider many factors when attempting to decide which child care service to use. Some of the most important factors include how many children each teacher or caregiver is in charge of, what qualifications the teachers or caregivers have, how long those teachers or caregivers have worked for the facility, and whether the facility is appropriately licensed and accredited. The number of children that a particular caregiver has to care for at one time, as well as how many children attend the facility, can play a large role in how much time a caregiver can devote to each child. A consumer should also verify that not only the facility itself is accredited and licensed, but also that the teachers or caregivers who work with the children have the knowledge and experience necessary to care for them.

While many resources are available to consumers seeking the best child care in their area, one of the best sources of information is usually the child care facility itself. By visiting child care centers under consideration, consumers can gather firsthand information about a particular facility, such as how many children the facility cares for at one time. A consumer should also be able to find information regarding the facility's accreditation while visiting

- 47 -

the facility and should later verify that the accreditation is valid and accurate. The Child Care Bureau, which is a subdivision of the United States Department of Health and Human Services, has services available to help consumers locate local organizations that will verify the accreditation of a child care provider. The Child Care Bureau can also be a useful resource for finding additional information about local child care programs.

Elder care services

The first step in the process of choosing a facility to care for an elderly family member is recognizing that the family member needs assistance beyond what the rest of the family can provide. After the family realizes that the elderly individual needs additional care, the second step is to evaluate the needs of the family member. By having a basic idea of what the elderly individual is capable of doing on his or her own and what he or she needs assistance with, a consumer will more effectively be able to research facilities that best suit the needs of the individual. The next step of the process involves gathering information regarding the appropriate facilities for the elderly individual. Finally, the family should choose the facility that appears to best suit those needs.

Knowing the needs of an elderly person and finding the elder care facility that best suits those needs is important because each elderly individual functions at a different level of ability. Because each person has different capabilities and needs, facilities should be evaluated on how well they are able to take care of the individual needs of each patient. Ensuring that an elderly individual is placed in the environment that allows him or her the most freedom and is the closest match to his or her current level of functioning is of utmost importance. For example, a woman who is capable of performing normal activities such as bathing, eating, and moving around on her own should not be placed in a nursing home. However, for a woman who has a high risk of injuring herself due to medical conditions, an assisted living home may be an appropriate option.

A consumer who is examining possibilities for the appropriate care facility for an elderly family member has the option of using resources available from the Administration on Aging. The Administration on Aging is a division of the Department of Health and Human Services that offers resources for locating local care facilities, as well as state and local agencies that monitor those facilities, so that consumers can get a better idea of what kinds of facilities are available. Another source of information available to consumers is the National Institute of Aging, an organization that provides a variety of publications regarding the needs and health concerns of elderly individuals. The National Institute of Aging also offers an online database for finding local care facilities. Regardless of which resources a consumer chooses to use, the best resource is often visiting the facilities in person to see what kind of services they can offer and what problems the facility might have.

Repair services

A consumer who is looking for a nearby repair service can find information about local repair shops, garages, and other repair services providers from the local Better Business Bureau. Each Better Business Bureau is comprised of a number of area businesses that are expected to uphold a certain standard of operation. In return, the Better Business Bureau suggests member businesses in good standing to consumers. If a consumer is considering using a repair service that belongs to a larger chain of stores, he or she might consult a publication such as *Consumer Reports* to discover if the chain has experienced problems or had complaints filed against them in the past. Even if these publications make the chain appear to be a good option, the consumer may still want to check with the local Better Business Bureau, as each store within a chain can often have its own problems and complaints that are separate from the chain itself.

Determining if an automobile, a child's toy, or other product is safe

The best resources that a consumer can use when attempting to determine if a product is safe are *Consumer Reports* magazine, the Consumer Product Safety Commission, and the National Fraud Information Center. In addition to offering a variety of reviews and information regarding the quality of most common products, *Consumer Reports* documents common defects and complaints that consumers have reported about those products. The Consumer Product Safety Commission offers consumers access to a number of publications regarding what to look for when inspecting products for defects. The Consumer Product Safety Commission also features listings of products that have already been recalled or have been shown to have potentially dangerous defects. The National Fraud Information Center can also be an important resource for evaluating the safety of a product, as it provides consumers information about products that businesses may have deliberately hidden or lied about in an attempt to make their products more appealing to consumers.

Creating a family budget

A family that has decided to create a family budget should begin by calculating how much money it has on hand and how much income it receives annually. Next, the family should determine what expenses it has and which of those expenses are necessary and which expenses are for luxuries. Necessary expenses might include housing, food, utilities, child care, health care, transportation, and insurance. Luxuries might include eating at restaurants, going to movies, buying a bigger television, getting manicures and pedicures, and other activities that are not necessary to the family's continued survival. The third step that a family should take when making a budget is to add up all of the total necessary expenses and subtract that total from the family's total annual income to find its total annual income after necessary expenses. Next, the family should decide how much of that money will be applied to the family's savings. Any remaining money can then be budgeted for less necessary items and activities.

Credit

Credit is the ability of a consumer to purchase a product or service now and pay for that product or service at a later time, either in full or in installments. Credit can be useful for consumers because it offers a way for handling larger expenses, such as the purchase of a house, when the consumer does not have enough funds on hand to make the purchase. However, consumers must keep track of the purchases they make with credit and realize that purchases made using credit must be paid back, usually with interest. If consumers fail to pay back the bank or credit card company that loaned them the money for the purchase or does not pay installments on time, their ability to get credit in the future is greatly impacted.

Some tactics that might be useful to consumers attempting to manage their credit more carefully include paying bills on time, avoiding purchases that they cannot afford, keeping track of how much debt they have, and carefully monitoring their credit report. Consumers who avoid making purchases that they cannot afford are much more likely to pay off loans on time, which will help keep their credit in good standing. If consumers make too many purchases, accumulate too much debt, or take out too many loans, they will most likely struggle to pay their bills. Extensive debt often indicates that consumers cannot manage their credit, which adversely affects their credit scores. Consumers should also closely monitor their credit reports so that they can dispute erroneous claims that may be negatively influencing their credit.

Investments and retirement plans

Investment is the process of committing an individual's resources to a particular activity, organization, or fund, with the hope that such a commitment will provide additional resources for the individual in the future. Investing and saving for retirement early in a person's career is important because careful investment planning guarantees that a person's financial resources have the opportunity to grow as much as possible. Individuals may have difficulty maintaining their customary standard of living if they do not have sufficient funds set aside when they retire because living expenses increase yearly. Individuals who do not have enough money set aside when they retire could become a burden to family members, as they may depend on the family to help support them financially.

Some of the factors that an individual or family might consider when making investment decisions are the risk of the investment, the potential return of the investment, and how difficult liquidating the investment would be. The risk of the investment refers to how likely it is that the individual or family will gain some benefit from the investment and how likely it is that the individual or family will lose the resources that they have invested. The potential return of the investment refers to how much money the individual or family will likely earn from the investment's interest or dividends over time. The degree of difficulty in cashing-out the investment is an important factor because different investments have different costs, taxes, lengths of time to mature, and stipulations regarding the access of the money associated with them.

Investments such as checking accounts, savings accounts, and CDs are considered low-risk investments, but they also offer a lower return. These investments are safe because banks guarantee that these accounts will earn a certain amount of interest; however, the rate of interest is relatively low in comparison with other investment options. While CDs are low-risk investments, they do offer slightly higher rates of interest than checking or savings accounts, but they can be liquidated only after they mature over a length of time set by the bank. Mutual funds are usually considered low-risk to mid-risk investments, as people have the potential to lose the resources they have invested, but mutual funds also have the potential to yield a higher return, though not as high as high-risk stocks. Because the stock portfolios that mutual funds are invested in are typically diversified and comprised of many different types of relatively stable stocks, mutual funds are generally regarded to be safe investments.

Families that are selecting what investments to make should first consider the financial goals that they hope to attain from these investments. For example, if a family is investing its resources to send family members to college, the family should estimate how much money it will need to pay for each member who plans to attend college. After a family has determined its financial needs, it can begin researching investment options to determine which investments are likely to yield enough financial gain for the family to reach its goals. Once it has identified which investments best suit its goals, the family should assess how much risk each investment carries. Finally, the family should choose the investment that has the lowest risk but will still meet its financial goals.

An individual who is attempting to determine how much money he or she needs to invest or put aside for retirement should start by adding up how much he or she spends monthly on living expenses, with the exception of health care. That number is then multiplied by 1.5, while health care expenses are multiplied by 2 to determine how much those expenses will increase in ten years. The individual then needs to estimate how many years he or she has before retirement; for every ten years, the health care expenses once again are multiplied by 2 and all other expenses by 1.5. Finally, adding these two results together equals an individual's estimated monthly expenses adjusted for inflation, thereby providing the individual with a rough estimate of how much he or she will need each month to maintain the same standard of living after retirement.

Insurance

The major types of insurance that an individual or family might need are health insurance, homeowner's insurance, life insurance, and car insurance. The reason that a family should have these types of insurance is that a problem in any of these areas can have a significant impact on the financial security of the individual or the family as a whole. Health problems, fire, theft, the death of a provider in the family, or a car accident can all lead to additional expenses that the individual or family may not be able to afford. Having these types of insurance offers individuals and families a way to pay unexpected expenses without significantly impacting their overall financial well-being.

Warranties

A warranty, also known as a guarantee, is a promise made by the seller of a product or service that the product or service will function as advertised or else the seller will attempt to repair or replace the product or perform the service again. Warranties usually apply only if the product or service fails to function when the consumer is using the product properly, and there are often many other conditions that must be met for the seller to carry out the terms of the warranty. Warranties are important to consumers because they offer a certain amount of protection against products that fail immediately or shortly after being purchased. However, because many warranties limit the types of repairs the seller is required to perform, consumers should be aware of the terms and conditions of a warranty before making a purchase.

Checking or savings account

An individual or family should consider several factors when opening a checking or savings account: What are the bank's minimum balance requirements? What bank fees are associated with the account? What is the annual interest rate earned by the account? Most banks charge account holders if they have less than the minimum balance required in their accounts. Banks often charge additional fees for ATM use and other services, which makes an account more expensive to the consumer than he or she might realize. If the financial institution charges a significant number of fees without offering a high interest rate on the account, the consumer should move his or her accounts to a different institution.

Consumers should also verify that a bank, credit union, or any other institution that they are considering placing money into is insured by the federal government through the Federal Deposit Insurance Corporation (FDIC) or the National Credit Union Administration (NCUA).

Product labels

Product labels are important, and sometimes vital, because they inform a consumer about the ingredients in a product, the materials used in the construction of a product, the appropriate way to use a product, and the hazards that can result from using a product incorrectly. This information can be useful for determining not only which products suit the needs of a consumer, but also if products are safe to use around children and other family members. For example, a label allows a consumer to determine if a particular piece of clothing is made out of a strong enough material for the consumer's intended use or if the material could trigger an allergic reaction in the consumer.

Nutritional needs

Some of the major factors that can affect an individual's nutritional needs include the age of the individual, the individual's gender, and his or her level of activity. The age of an individual plays a major role in the nutritional needs that person has in several ways. As a child grows, for instance, the number of calories the child needs also increases, but after the individual passes a certain age, the number of calories he or she needs decreases. A person's need for specific vitamins and minerals also increases as he or she gets older. Gender can affect an individual's nutritional needs; men typically require more protein and more calories than women do, while women usually require significantly more iron than men. The individual's level of activity also plays a large role in his or her nutritional needs because an individual who is more active will require a larger number of calories than an individual who less active.

Family and consumer education

Family and consumer education aims to improve a variety of skills that are essential for the day-to-day functioning of an individual and his or her family. Family and consumer education includes specific topics such as family interaction, human development, nutrition, consumer economics, types of housing and housing design, textiles, parenting, and the appropriate cooking and handling of foods. Family and consumer education covers both the physical and the psychological needs of the individual, and emphasizes appropriate social interaction between the individual and the rest of society.

Careers

Family and consumer science skills are useful in food management, financial management, human resources, public relations, tailoring, dress-making, etc. Indeed, regardless of career, an individual always finds a use for these skills in life. An individual in food management needs to know about nutrition and the proper handling and preparation of food. Financial advisors need to know how to assess resources, cut costs, and determine how much an individual needs to save before retirement. Human resource and public relations managers need social skills and training in time and resource management, human development, and psychology. Finally, tailors and dressmakers use their knowledge of textiles and textile design to create better garments.

In order to help students determine their interests and develop their skills, teachers should give them some example descriptions of various careers. Some of these examples may be family and consumer science careers, though it is not necessary for them all to be so. The class should examine a diverse sampling of different careers, especially since family and consumer science skills can be applied to virtually any setting. For example, a construction worker might not need to know about food, textiles, or housing design, but he or she still needs to know various problem-solving techniques. It can also be extremely useful for students to get some hands-on experience applying family and consumer science concepts to the tasks associated with different careers.

Work simplification

Work simplification is the process of discovering and implementing a series of procedures allowing an individual or a group of individuals to complete a task more easily and efficiently. Based on the particular type of task being performed, work can be simplified in a number of ways by determining the best possible way to complete a task without significantly impacting the overall quality of the work. Some of the basic methods used to make any task easier and more efficient include ensuring that individuals have access to necessary equipment, that work areas are organized, and that any steps in the work process that do not directly affect the outcome of the work are eliminated.

Community advisory committees

Community advisory committees can be extremely useful to an education professional who is attempting to determine what areas of the family and consumer science discipline a teaching plan should emphasize because the committees offer insight into the concerns and demographics of the students. Each community has its own problems, concerns, and level of diversity, and it is important that a family and consumer science teacher can recognize and focus on areas of concern in the school's community. For example, a community that is having problems with widespread teenage drug abuse and teenage suicide may want the community's family and consumer science teachers to focus more on the topic of avoiding substance abuse and the methods of handling depression. The goal of a family and consumer sciences educator is to improve the overall quality of life for the students and their families, and the educator cannot do that if he or she does not know what problems need to be addressed.

Some of the functions that community advisory committees perform, other than offering advice to education professionals, include assessing the performance of family and consumer science programs, assessing the performance of students with special needs, and providing equipment, technology, and resources for family and consumer science programs. These resources may include raw materials, textile samples, charts and diagrams, library books, and access to computers and design software. Community advisory committees also help students improve their chances of finding better jobs and careers and act as a public relations liaison for local family and consumer science programs. Ultimately, the primary purpose of a family and consumer sciences community advisory committee is to ensure that a family and consumer sciences program has all of the resources and training necessary to achieve the program's goals.

Balancing home and work roles

It is important that an individual is able to balance his or her work and home roles because it is becoming more and more common for individuals to have to act as both caregiver and provider for the family. The ever more common presence of dual roles in society can be extremely difficult for an individual to balance, as there may be instances where work-related responsibilities and family-related responsibilities conflict with one another. Family and consumer sciences education attempts to teach individuals how to avoid and how to handle these conflicts through the use of successful life management tactics such as time and resources management, problem-solving and decision-making techniques, and effective communication techniques. Family and consumer sciences education also attempts to give individuals a basic understanding of what responsibilities and qualities are necessary for the successful completion of each role so that individuals can set better priorities and find better ways to plan their lives.

Eliminating sexual stereotypes

Eliminating sexual stereotypes is a major concern of family and consumer sciences education. It is important for students to disregard sexual stereotypes and recognize that an individual's gender does not necessarily affect the role he or she plays. In the early- and mid-1900s, women were commonly seen as caretakers of the home and men as providers for the family. However, these roles have changed drastically over the past fifty to sixty years, and are not entirely realistic at this point. As the cost of living increases, it becomes more difficult for a single individual to provide for an entire family. As a result, it is more common for men and women to share the caretaker and provider roles to satisfy the physiological, financial, and psychological needs of the family.

Goals that family and consumer sciences education attempts to accomplish

The Association for Career and Technical Education has identified nine goals commonly associated with family and consumer sciences education. These nine goals include:
1. Improving the overall quality of life for individuals and families.
2. Helping individuals and families become responsible members of society.
3. Encouraging healthy eating habits, nutrition, and lifestyles.
4. Improve how individuals and families manage their resources.
5. Helping individuals and families balance their personal, family, and work lives.
6. Teaching individuals better problem-solving techniques.
7. Encouraging personal and career development.
8. Teaching individuals to successfully function as both consumers and providers.
9. Recognizing human worth and taking responsibility for one's own actions.

Improving the overall quality of life

The first of the nine goals established for family and consumer sciences education is to improve the overall quality of life for individuals and families, which is also the primary mission of all the goals. Family and consumer sciences education teaches people about how individuals, families, and the rest of society interact with each other, along with methods for improving those interactions. These methods include problem-solving techniques, common scams and problems to avoid, methods to stay healthy both physically and psychologically, and the distribution of a variety of other information regarding how the individual, family, and the rest of society function. Ultimately, family and consumer sciences education strives to improve the quality of life by educating individuals and families in the best manner to function on a day-to-day basis. However, this goal is truly accomplished only when the other eight goals of family and consumer sciences education are met as well.

Basic concepts

There are several concepts at the core of family and consumer education, but one of the most important concepts is that families form the basic unit of society. Another important concept of family and consumer education is that individuals need to be life-long learners in order to develop and function successfully. Finally, family and consumer education promotes the idea that individuals and families need to have an understanding of the advantages of experimenting with different decision-making methods and diverse ways of thinking in order to solve any given problem.

Characteristics of occupational family and consumer sciences education

Occupational family and consumer sciences education is a teaching discipline that is similar to the standard discipline of family and consumer education but focuses less on the skills for day-to-day living and more on how those skills can be used in the workplace. Occupational family and consumer sciences education covers information regarding skills that can commonly be applied in fields such as health services, food service, child care, hospitality, fashion design, interior design, and many other similar fields. Occupational family and consumer sciences education places more emphasis on family and consumer skills that directly relate to a career, such as management techniques and ethical businesses practices, than the standard family and consumer education discipline. The occupational family and consumer sciences education discipline ultimately takes the skills that an individual has learned from the standard discipline and shows how those skills can be applied to a career.

Laboratory settings

A laboratory setting is important for an educator teaching family and consumer sciences because it offers students an opportunity to gain hands-on experience using a variety of skills and techniques. Many important areas of the family and consumer sciences discipline center around using a combination of various skills to achieve a certain end result and sometimes the best way to teach the appropriate way to integrate these skills is through experience. A laboratory setting offers students a place to demonstrate and improve their skills related to the family and consumer science field with the advantage of having a teacher present to answer questions and correct mistakes. Some examples of useful laboratory settings for the family and consumer sciences field include kitchens or food science laboratories, day care centers, and testing laboratories for textiles and consumer products.

Demonstrating family and consumer science concepts

There are a large number of methods that an educator can use to demonstrate concepts related to family and consumer sciences, but the best methods always involve promoting students' active participation. Some examples of active participation include allowing students to use a sewing machine; having students test the qualities of various textiles to see how soft, lustrous, resilient, absorbent, etc. each material is; and requiring students to prepare a meal. Students can also demonstrate active participation with the following activities: comparing advertisements to find the best offer for a particular product, examining common marketing tactics, visiting or working in a local daycare center, and being involved in local community service activities. Many of these activities serve not only as effective ways of teaching students about the important concepts of family and consumer sciences, but also as a means of testing the students' ability to apply the techniques, skills, and information that they have learned.

Professional organizations

Professional organizations such as the American Association of Family and Consumer Sciences, also known as the AAFCS, play an important role in influencing the education of individuals in the methodology and knowledge associated with family and consumer sciences. Many of these local and national professional organizations offer seminars, courses, and publications on a wide range of topics directly to individuals and families to teach them about essential career and management skills, how to be smart consumers, the importance of following nutritional guidelines, and information about a wide range of other topics. These professional organizations also provide publications, advice, and curriculum guides to educational professionals that help these professionals teach and stay informed regarding important changes to the curriculum that result from changes in legislation, society, and the education system itself. These organizations also have a profound effect on family and consumer science education by influencing public policy and gathering support for programs that help educate and protect individuals and families from unsafe habits, business practices, products, and lifestyles.

FCCLA

The FCCLA, which stands for the Family, Career, and Community Leaders of America, is a youth organization for students in family and consumer science education. The FCCLA offers a variety of publications and programs designed to educate people about parenting, relationships, substance abuse, teen pregnancy, and teen violence, among other concerns. By focusing public attention to the problems that young people face, the FCCLA gains support for programs and laws that help protect young people and their families. The FCCLA also shows students how they can improve their family and consumer science skills and apply those skills later in life.

The FCCLA and other similar youth organizations play an important role in influencing national policy related to protecting families and consumers. Additionally, these organizations are important because they support family and consumer science educational programs, which strive to improve the overall quality of life for individuals and families by teaching people skills that will enable them to live better lives.

Legislation

When a new act of legislation is passed, it can often have a profound impact on the types of materials used in family and consumer sciences classrooms, as well as the issues that should be addressed by family and consumer sciences education. It is important that individuals understand the legal protections and rights granted to them by the various acts put into place by state and federal governments. Since laws are constantly changing, family and consumer science educators must be able to adapt quickly and add information regarding new legislation to their curriculum.

Determining whether a student understands a particular concept

Usually, the best method an educator can use to verify whether a student understands a particular concept is to see if the student can actively apply the information he or she has learned to such everyday tasks as cooking, sewing, and time management; however, a student may not be able to demonstrate his or her understanding of certain concepts if a laboratory setting is not available. Alternative methods by which an educator can evaluate a student's level of comprehension include administering written tests, assigning projects and research papers, teaching students to design charts and diagrams, involving students in the evaluation of case studies and scenarios, and requiring students keep a journal of their activities and eating habits. Which evaluation method an educator should use depends primarily on the curriculum being covered and the abilities of the students who are taking the class.

Meeting the special needs of a student

The first step an educator should take when determining the best way to meet the special needs of a student is to identify exactly what that particular child's needs consist of, as each student is unique in his or her ability to learn and comprehend. If a student is performing poorly, a teacher must determine the cause of the student's poor performance. Once the cause has been identified, the teacher can then determine how much assistance the student needs. If the student's needs can be met through such techniques as one-on-one attention or special project assignments, this is usually the best course of action. However, if the student has needs that require solutions beyond simple changes in curriculum, including potential psychological or physiological disorders, the educator has an obligation to consult with other educational professionals and to discuss other options with the child's parents.

Affective skill, cognitive skill and psychomotor skill

Affective skill refers to how effectively an individual can recognize, understand, and handle emotions and relationships. Affective skills allow an individual to feel appropriate emotion in response to certain situations or stimuli, and then to respond appropriately.

Cognitive skill refers to an individual's ability to gather and understand information. Cognitive skills allow an individual to comprehend new situations and apply the knowledge that he or she has gathered elsewhere.

Psychomotor skill refers to an individual's ability to coordinate his or her physical movements. In other words, psychomotor skills are a person's control over simple and complex motor functions.

It is extremely important for an individual to be able to use a combination of his or her affective, cognitive, and psychomotor skills together on a day-to-day basis, as each type of skill is essential to the overall functioning of a healthy individual. An individual who has mastered his or her psychomotor skills may be in excellent physical health, but the individual's emotional and intellectual health will suffer if he or she is unable to make effective relationships and understand basic and complex concepts. The situation is the

- 57 -

same for individuals who can only maintain effective relationships or who can only understand complex concepts, as it will be significantly more difficult for them to perform everyday functions if they have poor control of their psychomotor skills. For an individual to maintain his or her physical and mental health, along with that of his or her family, the individual must be able to use a combination of different skills.

Some of the factors that can be used to measure how well-developed an individual's affective skills are include determining how well the individual receives emotional stimuli and how well the individual responds to those stimuli. It is also important to determine how easy it is for the individual to acknowledge the worth of a particular situation, relationship, or individual and whether the individual has an organized and well-conceived value system. An individual's ability to receive and respond to emotional stimuli can be measured by how aware the individual is of a particular stimulus, how willing the individual is to acknowledge that particular stimulus, and how focused the individual is on that stimulus. An individual's ability to assign value to a situation and uphold a value system can be measured by how motivated the individual is, how the individual behaves, and how consistent that individual's behavior is. For example, a student that always comes to class and clearly always pays attention may have well-developed affective skills.

Some of the factors that can be used to measure how well-developed an individual's cognitive skills are include determining the individual's ability to retain knowledge, comprehend knowledge, apply knowledge, and evaluate knowledge. An individual's ability to retain knowledge can be measured by testing the individual's ability to remember certain facts and information through exams or simply asking questions. An individual's ability to comprehend knowledge can be measured by an individual demonstrating a concept in a different form, explaining a concept in more detail or simplifying a concept, or predicting a result based on a particular concept. An individual breaking a concept down into individual parts and demonstrating how those parts make up the whole can also show comprehension of a particular concept. An individual's ability to apply knowledge can be measured by an individual demonstrating that they can use a particular concept for a real-life purpose. Finally, an individual's ability to evaluate a particular piece of knowledge can be indicated by the individual showing the value of that knowledge.

Some of the factors that can be used to measure how well-developed an individual's psychomotor skills are include how well an individual performs physical skills and acts, how precisely can the individual perform those skills or activities, and how natural do those activities seem to be for the individual. An individual's ability to use physical skills can be measured simply by how much difficulty the individual has in accomplishing a particular complex physical activity such as climbing a rope or assembling a model. How precisely the individual can perform those skills or activities can be measured by determining the quality of the result of the individual's physical activity and how long it took the individual to reach that result. For example, if the individual has constructed a model plane, does the model look like a plane, are its wings and other parts attached correctly, how long it took to assemble, etc. Finally, an activity is natural for an individual if the individual can perform it without thinking.

Practice Test

Practice Questions

1. The process through which a person comes to think of himself or herself as a distinct person despite being a member of a family is known as
    a. collectivization.
    b. individuation.
    c. personalization.
    d. ego birth.
    e. personification.

2. In which kind of society are people more likely to live with their extended families?
    a. Modern
    b. Industrial
    c. Urban
    d. Agrarian
    e. Nomadic

3. Which of the following is NOT considered to be necessary for a person to commit emotionally to a marriage?
    a. Good self-esteem
    b. Empathy
    c. A feeling of permanence
    d. Financial stability
    e. A strong personal identity

4. Which of the following factors has no effect on job satisfaction?
    a. Having a child between the ages of 2 and 4
    b. Flexible scheduling
    c. Parenting a newborn
    d. High wages
    e. Intellectual challenge

5. What is the first step a person should take after divorce?
    a. Receive justice from the former spouse
    b. Achieve balance between being single and being a parent
    c. Accept the fact that the marriage is over
    d. Develop goals for the future
    e. Begin looking for a new partner

6. For which pair would sibling rivalry likely be greatest?
    a. Sister and brother, ages 5 and 10, respectively
    b. Sisters, ages 10 and 5
    c. Brother and sister, ages 8 and 10, respectively
    d. Brothers, ages 3 and 5

7. Which of the following statements about marriage is false?
    a. Married men are less likely to abuse alcohol.
    b. Married women typically earn higher wages than single women.
    c. On average, married women are healthier than single women.
    d. People who have been married in the past are more likely to marry again than people who have never married.
    e. More than 90% of Americans will marry at some point.

8. In general, accepting a stepparent is hardest for
    a. preschoolers.
    b. girls around the age of eight.
    c. boys around the age of nine.
    d. adolescent boys.
    e. adolescent girls.

9. Which of the following statements about families is false?
    a. The content rather than the style of family communication is important.
    b. Families tend to make decisions that maintain the current state of affairs.
    c. Members of a family are likely to struggle with the same sorts of problems in life.
    d. Families change in response to pressures from the environment.
    e. It is impossible to understand the members of a family without understanding the family as a whole.

10. According to John Gottman, which of the following is the best response to criticism by a spouse?
    a. Defensiveness
    b. Stonewalling
    c. Reasoned argument
    d. Humor
    e. Acceptance

11. The greatest amount of variation between people of the same age is found during
    a. Infancy
    b. Early adolescence
    c. Early childhood
    d. Adulthood
    e. Late adolescence

12. When two children have a dispute and agree to settle it according to their mother's opinion, they are engaging in
    a. Arbitration
    b. Conciliation
    c. Mediation
    d. Negotiation
    e. Restorative justice

13. In general, when a mother works,
    a. her daughters are less independent.
    b. her unsupervised sons are less successful at school.
    c. her children have more self-esteem.
    d. it is not important for both parents to have a positive attitude about the arrangement.
    e. she is less satisfied with her life.

14. Which of the following is an assumption of structured family therapy?
    a. The life of a family is a series of actions and reactions.
    b. Family members tend to become locked in their roles.
    c. During times of conflict, family members will take sides to consolidate power.
    d. Bad behavior persists when it is reinforced.
    e. Family problems are caused by negative projection.

15. What is one drawback of inpatient treatment for alcoholism?
    a. It is rarely effective.
    b. It does not include a twelve-step program.
    c. It enables the patient to continue drinking while receiving treatment.
    d. It is expensive.
    e. It requires a personal commitment from the patient.

16. According to Piaget's model, the ability to imagine the mental lives of others emerges during the
    a. formal operational stage.
    b. concrete operational stage.
    c. primary socialization stage.
    d. preoperational stage.
    e. sensorimotor stage.

17. Role strain is exemplified by
    a. a public speaker who cultivates her expertise.
    b. a new teacher who struggles to maintain authority in the classroom.
    c. a person whose parents die.
    d. a child who imagines what it would be like to be a police officer.
    e. a substitute teacher who waits tables on the weekend.

18. Which of the following people is most likely to have an IQ of 125?
    a. A fourteen year-old with the mental age of a ten year-old
    b. A five year-old with the mental age of an eight year-old
    c. A ten year-old with the mental age of a seven year-old
    d. An eight year-old with the mental age of a twelve year-old
    e. An eight year-old with the mental age of a ten year-old

19. A student whose interest level and performance have steadily declined admits to his teacher that he is depressed. Unfortunately, the student is not yet willing to do anything to remedy this problem. In which stage of the transtheoretical model of change is this student?
    a. Action
    b. Maintenance
    c. Preparation/commitment
    d. Contemplation
    e. Precontemplation

20. Starting at about nine months, an infant will begin nonsensically imitating adult speech, a process known as
    a. telegraphic speech.
    b. holophrastic speech.
    c. cooing.
    d. deep structuring.
    e. echolalia.

21. What is the major criticism of Levinson's "seasons" of life model?
    a. It overstates the importance of the mid-life crisis.
    b. It is too idealized.
    c. It ignores the last years of life.
    d. It suggests that life transitions are made unconsciously.
    e. It discounts the influence of parents.

22. Which of the following is NOT a warning sign of teen depression?
    a. Sudden interest in a new hobby
    b. Aloofness
    c. Fatigue
    d. A change in sleep patterns
    e. Rapid weight change

23. Students who excel in math receive different treatment than students who excel in English. This is an example of
    a. vertical socialization.
    b. horizontal socialization.
    c. resocialization.
    d. anticipatory socialization.
    e. desocialization.

24. Which of the following is NOT one of the areas of emotional intelligence?
    a. Self-awareness
    b. Empathy
    c. Personal motivation
    d. Thrift
    e. Altruism

25. Which of the following statements about teen pregnancy is false?
    a. The United States has the lowest rate of teen pregnancy in North America.
    b. The rate of teen pregnancy is higher among Hispanics and African-Americans.
    c. Teenage mothers are less likely to complete high school.
    d. Teen pregnancy rates have decreased over the past twenty years.
    e. Teenage parents earn less money over the course of their lives.

26. An effective time management plan
    a. encourages students to do their most difficult tasks first.
    b. eliminates every possible distraction.
    c. includes time for meals.
    d. eschews lists.
    e. will be the same for every student.

27. Creating a list of things to do is less necessary
    a. when children are teething.
    b. when both parents work in the home.
    c. when a daily routine has been established.
    d. when children are in school.
    e. when both parents work outside the home.

28. Which of Hersey and Blanchard's leadership styles emphasizes the performance of tasks and ignores the development of positive relationships?
    a. Selling
    b. Delegating
    c. Supporting
    d. Telling
    e. Participating

29. What is the best method for a family to decide on a vacation destination?
    a. One parent decides
    b. Ideas are thrown into a hat and selected at random
    c. Children decide
    d. Discussion, then a final decision by parents
    e. Vote

30. The best way to limit a child's television time is to
    a. take away privileges until the child submits.
    b. tell the child that television will rot his brain.
    c. ignore the issue.
    d. suggest that the child go outside.
    e. set a timer and turn the television off when the alarm sounds.

31. A group will often make more extreme decisions than any one member would make independently. This phenomenon is known as
    a. organizational conflict.
    b. group polarization.
    c. social facilitation.
    d. groupthink.
    e. social loafing.

32. The members of a family are more likely to be motivated when
   a. they are forced to commit to a goal.
   b. a goal is well defined.
   c. they believe that their work is inherently good, regardless of any tangible reward.
   d. they do not evaluate their own performance.
   e. they feel as if they are working harder than other members.

33. A compressed workweek
   a. decreases the amount of time spent at work every day.
   b. is made up of 5 eight-hour days.
   c. improves employee satisfaction.
   d. tends to diminish performance.
   e. is especially beneficial for employees who work at home.

34. What is the first step a person should take toward eliminating wasted time?
   a. Keeping a log of how time is spent
   b. Resolving to sleep less
   c. Purchasing efficient home appliances
   d. Using an egg timer
   e. Focusing on one's most important tasks

35. A five year-old is probably too young to
   a. clean up spills with a sponge.
   b. sweep a wooden floor.
   c. dust shelves.
   d. mop the kitchen floor.
   e. put away toys.

36. The proper decision-making process begins by
   a. defining the problem to be solved.
   b. listing various solutions.
   c. researching potential solutions.
   d. assembling a team to solve the problem.
   e. estimating the cost of solving the problem.

37. When making a schedule, children should be encouraged to
   I. include some free time.
   II. place the hardest tasks first.
   III. block out long stretches for completing all homework.
   a. I only
   b. II only
   c. III only
   d. I and II
   e. II and III

38. Drop-in child care is useful when
    a. parents have very little money.
    b. a family's regular child care provider is unavailable.
    c. a family is away from home.
    d. a child has special needs.
    e. a child is in school.

39. What is one disadvantage of dealing with consumer finance companies?
    a. They do not loan money for very many purposes.
    b. They provide different rates of interest depending on the client's credit record.
    c. They help consumers purchase goods they could not otherwise afford.
    d. They tend to charge high interest rates.
    e. They do not accept property as security.

40. What type of business is the most common employer of high-school students?
    a. Grocery stores
    b. Movie theaters
    c. Theme parks
    d. Clothing stores
    e. Restaurants

41. Borrowers with a poor credit rating will not be eligible for a bank's
    a. prime rate.
    b. savings deposits.
    c. demand deposits.
    d. deposit insurance.
    e. certificates of deposit.

42. Which of the following statements about daycare is true?
    a. Children in daycare tend to be less aggressive.
    b. It is not necessary to establish the parent-child bond before beginning daycare.
    c. Children not in daycare tend to make friends more easily.
    d. The value of daycare is not related to the quality of the supervision.
    e. Children in daycare are better at articulating their desires.

43. Which of the following was NOT one of the consumer rights asserted by Presidents Kennedy and Nixon during the 1960s?
    a. Right to a safe product
    b. Right to affordability
    c. Right to redress
    d. Right to be heard
    e. Right to be informed

44. According to personal finance experts, what is the maximum percentage of income a family should spend on housing?
    a. 5%
    b. 50%
    c. 10%
    d. 25%
    e. 35%

45. Which of the following represents a discretionary expense?
    a. Textbook
    b. Rent
    c. DVD
    d. Groceries
    e. Heating oil

46. What is the typical interval for a personal budget?
    a. One day
    b. One week
    c. One month
    d. Six months
    e. One year

47. Denise has a credit card with an APR of 4.5%. If she has an average balance of $2500 throughout the year, how much interest will accrue?
    a. $25.00
    b. $112.50
    c. $450.00
    d. $450.50
    e. $2612.50

48. It is NOT a good idea to
    a. allow a child to visit a daycare center before his or her first official day there.
    b. ask daycare providers how toilet training is handled.
    c. allow a child to bring his favorite blanket or stuffed animal to daycare.
    d. visit less than three daycare providers before selecting one.
    e. have a positive discussion with a child who is about to begin daycare.

49. Which type of corporate bond is secured only by the assets and earnings of the corporation?
    a. Collateral trust bond
    b. Mortgage bond
    c. Sinking-fund bond
    d. Convertible bond
    e. Debenture bond

50. What is the major benefit of vitamin A?
    a. It helps form new cells.
    b. It helps protect the body from disease.
    c. It can increase a person's concentration and alertness.
    d. It can give a person healthy hair and skin.
    e. It enables muscle contraction.

51. Which food group has a recommended daily intake of two and half cups?
    a. Grains
    b. Dairy
    c. Fruits
    d. Vegetables
    e. Protein foods

52. The daily values listed on food packaging assume that
    a. the food will be shared between two people.
    b. the food will not be cooked.
    c. a person's daily diet consists of two thousand calories.
    d. the product contains preservatives.
    e. the product is unspoiled.

53. In order to reduce the risk of spinal bifida in infants, food manufacturers have begun adding
    a. calcium.
    b. folic acid.
    c. iron.
    d. vitamin K.
    e. magnesium.

54. Which of the following events decreases metabolism?
    a. Rapid weight loss
    b. Increase in muscle mass
    c. Slow weight gain
    d. Moderate workout
    e. Rapid weight gain

55. An ovo-lacto-vegetarian is a person who eats
    a. Fruits, vegetables, and grains
    b. Fruits, vegetables, grains, and poultry
    c. Fruits, vegetables, grains, and dairy products
    d. Fruits, vegetables, grains, dairy products, and eggs
    e. Fruits, vegetables, grains, and eggs

56. Sodium and chloride are major minerals; every day a person should consume ___ of each.
    a. 100 milligrams
    b. 1 kilogram
    c. 10 milligrams
    d. 10 grams
    e. 1 gram

57. Which of the following vitamins is water-soluble?
    a. Vitamin D
    b. Vitamin E
    c. Vitamin K
    d. Vitamin A
    e. Vitamin C

58. What is one problem associated with the over-consumption of protein?
    a. Dehydration
    b. Increased muscle mass
    c. Strained liver and kidneys
    d. Heart palpitations
    e. Dandruff

59. Which kind of oil is NOT an unsaturated fat?
    a. Corn oil
    b. Olive oil
    c. Canola oil
    d. Palm oil
    e. Sunflower oil

60. The amount of energy required to raise the temperature of one gram of water by one degree Celsius is a(n)
    a. joule.
    b. calorie.
    c. ohm.
    d. microgram.
    e. watt.

61. A person who is 41 to 100% heavier than his or her ideal weight is
    a. mildly obese.
    b. osteoporotic.
    c. diabetic.
    d. moderately obese.
    e. severely obese.

62. Which of the following statements is true?
        I. Bulimia can lead to tooth decay.
        II. Anorexics tend to have a distorted self-image.
        III. Bulimia does not always include purging.
    a. I only
    b. II only
    c. III only
    d. I and II only
    e. I, II, and III

63. Which nutrient is not present in high levels in dairy products?
    a. Vitamin B-12
    b. Iron
    c. Protein
    d. Vitamin A
    e. Calcium

64. Which of the following vitamins is known to improve the body's ability to use phosphorus and calcium?
    a. Vitamin E
    b. Vitamin D
    c. Vitamin B-3
    d. Vitamin K
    e. Vitamin A

65. Which of the following statements about stain removal is true?
    a. Stained garments can be safely ironed.
    b. A fresh stain can be cleaned with bar soap.
    c. Milk stains should be treated with hot water.
    d. Regular clothing can be washed alongside clothing with chemical stains.
    e. Stained clothing should be cleaned within 24 hours.

66. Which fabrication method, typical of outerwear, involves stitching a liner fabric in between two outer fabrics?
    a. Knitting
    b. Stitch-through
    c. Quilting
    d. Tufting
    e. Weaving

67. What is the name for wool that has been spun into a fine yarn from parallel threads?
    a. Worsted
    b. Cashmere
    c. Angora
    d. Polyester
    e. Spandex

68. Fuzzy fibers that ball up and adhere to the outside of a garment are said to be
    a. fuzzing.
    b. snagging.
    c. breathing.
    d. pilling.
    e. creasing.

69. What does the word *carded* mean when it appears on a clothing label?
    a. The garment has been evaluated by a licensed inspector.
    b. The garment is made of short and thick cotton fibers.
    c. The garment was not created in a sweat shop.
    d. The garment only contains one type of fiber.
    e. The garment is resistant to wrinkles.

70. Which of the following garments would be the most resistant to wrinkles?
    a. Rayon jacket
    b. Cotton t-shirt
    c. Silk shirt
    d. Linen pants
    e. Wool pants

71. What is one common problem with silk clothing?
    a. It is easily damaged by the sun.
    b. It is very susceptible to abrasions.
    c. It has a tendency to wrinkle.
    d. It is very flammable.
    e. It is coarse.

72. The FTC does NOT mandate that clothing labels include
    a. the country of origin.
    b. whether the garment contains mink or rabbit.
    c. an indication of whether wool is new or recycled.
    d. the Registered Identification Number or name of the manufacturer.
    e. each fiber class represented in the item.

73. On which of the following fabrics is it safe to use bleach occasionally?
    a. Spandex
    b. Silk
    c. Cotton
    d. Wool
    e. Cashmere

74. Which fabric is best for blocking sunlight?
    a. Green satin
    b. Black cotton
    c. White cotton
    d. Black satin
    e. Red cotton

75. In interior design, the arrangement of elements in a pattern around some central point is known as
    a. symmetrical balance.
    b. gradation balance.
    c. asymmetrical balance.
    d. harmonic balance.
    e. radial balance.

76. In which layout pattern are spaces arranged along a linear path, with major elements at either end?
    a. Radial layout
    b. Dumbbell layout
    c. Clustered layout
    d. Doughnut layout
    e. Centralized layout

77. Which of the following represents the Fibonacci sequence?
    a. 0, 1, 1, 2, 3, 5...
    b. 0, 1, 2, 4, 8, 16...
    c. 0, 1, 1.5., 2, 2.5...
    d. 0, 1, 3, 6, 9, 12...
    e. 0, 2, 4, 6, 8, 10...

78. Which of the following is considered to be the most important determinant of human comfort in housing?
    a. Relative humidity
    b. Mean radiant temperature
    c. Air temperature
    d. Air quality
    e. Ventilation

79. Fabric hung across the window by a rod that covers either the extreme ends of the window or the entire window is called a
    a. curtain.
    b. louvered shutter.
    c. drapery.
    d. grille.
    e. Roman shade.

80. A kitchen is fourteen feet long and ten feet wide, but it has an adjoining pantry four feet deep and four feet wide. What is the gross area of the kitchen?
    a. 24 square feet
    b. 32 square feet
    c. 140 square feet
    d. 156 square feet
    e. 2240 square feet

81. The synthetic woodwork finish that creates the most durable surface is
    a. lacquer.
    b. polyurethane.
    c. varnish.
    d. vinyl.
    e. polyester.

82. Which of the following is NOT a good strategy for instructing a learning-disabled student?
    a. Breaking a complicated problem into simple steps
    b. Encouraging students to strive for perfection
    c. Establishing a daily routine
    d. Incorporating movement and tactile instruction whenever possible
    e. Delivering abstract concepts through dialogue with students

83. Which of the following is a cognitive objective of consumer science?
    a. Ability to select drapes
    b. Ability to arrange furniture
    c. Ability to load a shopping cart
    d. Ability to restrain consumer impulses
    e. Ability to create a personal budget

84. What is one common criticism of cooperative education programs?
    a. They isolate students from the rest of the academic community.
    b. They do not provide on-the-job training.
    c. They do not help students make career choices.
    d. They separate the business and academic communities.
    e. They decrease student motivation.

85. Which of the following is NOT one of the focuses of Junior Achievement programs at the high school level?
    a. Personal finance
    b. Business and entrepreneurship
    c. Community service
    d. Work preparation
    e. Economics

86. What is the primary focus of the FCCLA?
    a. College admission
    b. Academic achievement
    c. The family
    d. Career advancement
    e. Consumer education

87. A needs assessment for a family and consumer science program should begin with
    a. a gap analysis.
    b. lesson plans.
    c. prioritization.
    d. time management analysis.
    e. a survey of summative assessment results.

88. Which of the following is NOT a necessary component of an effective syllabus?
    a. Grading scale
    b. Mission statement
    c. List of community resources
    d. Clear assessment objectives
    e. Course content

89. A lesson plan calls for students to act out a negotiating scenario in which pairs of students try to settle a hypothetical dispute between a husband and wife over money. Which learning disability might prevent a student from succeeding at this task?
    a. Dyssemia
    b. Apraxia
    c. Dysgraphia
    d. Dyslexia
    e. Visual perception disorder

90. When evaluating Internet research, what is the least important consideration?
    a. Whether the website has an editorial board
    b. The organization that maintains the website
    c. The presence of links to similar websites
    d. The last time the website was updated
    e. An affiliation with the United States government

91. Many high-school students believe that the most important content area in family and consumer science is
    a. housing.
    b. the family.
    c. consumer science.
    d. personal finance.
    e. food and nutrition.

92. The original purpose of family and consumer science education was to
    a. redress social problems such as child labor and the repression of women.
    b. improve women's housekeeping skills.
    c. encourage frugality during the World War II.
    d. reinforce traditional family roles.
    e. encourage the use of household appliances.

93. Which of the following activities would best develop the psychomotor skills of elementary-school students?
    a. Learning to calculate compound interest
    b. Creating a budget for their school wardrobe
    c. Looking up banking terms in the dictionary
    d. Setting up a mock storefront for a retail business
    e. Drawing a picture of their ideal house

94. Name one advantage of large classes.
    a. Close relations between students and teacher
    b. Greater access to resources
    c. Expanded range of teaching methods
    d. Less record-keeping
    e. Greater comfort for the teacher

95. Which of the following is NOT a relevant factor when making changes in the family and consumer sciences curriculum?
   a. Experience
   b. Knowledge
   c. Time
   d. Skill
   e. Expense

96. A teacher is dividing the class up into groups for a project. What is the best way to avoid gender discrimination?
   a. Segregate the groups by gender.
   b. Encourage boys to include girls when making decisions.
   c. Encourage girls to handle tasks related to math.
   d. Be sure each group is comprised of both boys and girls.
   e. Give leadership positions to at least one boy and one girl in each group.

97. The primary determinant of whether a teacher will adopt instructional technology is
   a. estimated cost.
   b. student interest.
   c. perceived usefulness.
   d. the teacher's aptitude.
   e. geographic location.

98. The Carl D. Perkins Improvement Act of 2006 mandated that
   a. children with disabilities be given a free lunch.
   b. the curriculum of family and consumer science be aligned with general content standards.
   c. family and consumer science teachers obtain an undergraduate degree.
   d. students in family and consumer sciences pass a written examination.
   e. family and consumer sciences teachers focus on career training.

99. An activity that requires students to describe their ideal home falls within the
   a. psychomotor domain.
   b. analytic domain.
   c. cognitive domain.
   d. affective domain.
   e. synthetic domain.

100. Children between the ages of six and eight should be able to
   a. make change.
   b. compare the prices of products.
   c. maintain spending records.
   d. use the terminology associated with banking.
   e. count coins.

Answers and Explanations

1. B: Individuation is the process through which a person comes to think of himself or herself as a distinct person despite membership in a family. The development of children in a family can be seen as an ongoing process of individuation. Children at first identify entirely with the mores, norms, and values of their family; it is only after prolonged exposure to other people outside the home that a child will begin to question his or her upbringing and perhaps modify his or her belief system. A fully individualized person is able to maintain a coherent personality without necessarily renouncing membership in a family with which he or she may have some disagreement.

2. D: People who live in an agrarian society are more likely to live with their extended family. An extended family is comprised of more than one adult couple. For instance, it might include a man and a woman, their children, and their grandchildren. Agrarian societies in which people tend the same land for their entire lives are more conducive to the maintenance of the extended family. This is in part because it is more difficult for a large group to move around together. In modern, industrial, urban, and nomadic societies, it is more common for people to be grouped together in nuclear families. A nuclear family includes one adult couple and their children.

3. D: Financial stability is not one of the factors necessary for a person to commit emotionally to a marriage. This fact is interesting, since money is one of the main issues leading many divorces. However, many experts agree that it is much more important for partners to have good self-esteem, empathy, a feeling of permanence in the relationship, and strong personal identities. Solid marriages weather the inevitable hard times with a mixture of humor, empathy, and habit. The idea of empathy is particularly important in marriage because it implies that each partner may not fully understand the other. Nevertheless, a loving spouse will try to help whenever possible.

4. A: Having a young child has no measurable effect on job satisfaction. Curiously, this is true for both men and women. Research suggests that parents often feel some strain as they occupy multiple roles, but this is offset by the enjoyment they derive from their work. Having a newborn, on the other hand, has a noticeably damaging effect on job satisfaction. The demands of caring for a newborn, as well as the desire to spend as much time as possible with this new child, make it unpleasant to be away from home for any reason. Flexible scheduling, high wages, and intellectual challenge are all directly correlated with job satisfaction.

5. C: After divorce, the first step a person should take is to accept that the divorce is final and the marriage is over. This is easier said than done, as psychologists estimate that it takes most people at least two years to accept divorce entirely. Until this is reached, the divorcee should not initiate a new relationship. The best way to complete the process of acceptance is to establish an individual identity. This may include developing a balance between being single and being a parent. It is appropriate to plan for the future, but people should be aware that it is impossible to predict what they will want once they have fully processed the finality of the divorce.

6. D: Of the given pairs, sibling rivalry would likely be greatest for brothers aged 3 and 5. In general, sibling rivalry is most pronounced in same-sex siblings within three years of age. In the first eight to ten years of life, siblings tend to alternate between cooperation and competition. As they grow older, they will often spend little time together for a few years, but during adolescence will gradually develop empathy for one another. Most research suggests that adult relationships between siblings simply exaggerate the tone of the relationship of youth; that is, good relationships get better and bad relationships get worse.

7. B: Married women typically earn a lower wage than single women. This is an exception to the general trend, which is that married people are healthier, wealthier, and more content than their single counterparts. Married men are less likely to abuse alcohol and drugs, and less likely to become depressed. Married women are healthier and more likely to report satisfaction with their home lives. One reason why married women may earn less money is that they are more likely to be raising children, and therefore less focused on professional development. Despite reports about the decline of marriage, an overwhelming majority of Americans will marry at least once during their lives.

8. E: In general, accepting a stepparent is hardest for adolescent girls. Of course, this process is not easy for sons and daughters of any age. However, research suggests that the bond between a stepparent, in particular a stepfather, and an adolescent girl takes the longest to form. One possible reason for this phenomenon is that stepfathers tend to be less engaged with stepdaughters than with stepsons. The effect of remarriage on children is much the same as divorce because it involves a fundamental restructuring of the family concept. Nevertheless, stepparents who work to engage with their stepchildren can develop positive relationships over time.

9. A: Both the content and the style of family communication are important. For instance, a parent may deliver a positive message and then undermine it by demonstrating contrary behavior. The members of a family should work on communicating positively. The other answer choices are true statements about families. The decisions made by families tend to reinforce the status quo in the interest of conformity and conflict avoidance. For reasons both genetic and environmental, the members of families are likely to struggle with the same sorts of problems in life. Despite a general tendency toward stability and consistency, families inevitably change in response to the aging of each member and to pressures from the environment. Finally, it is a central tenet of family science that it is impossible to understand a family member without understanding the family as a whole.

10. D: According to John Gottman, the best response to criticism by a spouse is humor. Gottman has performed extensive research on the interactions between married couples and has identified characteristics of both durability and divorce. When the criticized partner responds to criticism by deflecting or soothing the other person, tempers are quelled and the partnership remains strong. Gottman's research suggests that there is a classic pattern of degenerating communication in an unsuccessful relationship. The pattern begins with criticism that is not directed at a certain behavior, but at the other person as a whole. In other words, the criticism of unsuccessful couples tends to lean toward character assassination. Eventually, these negative interactions lead to contempt, in which one partner openly disparages and disrespects the other. The inevitable response to contempt is defensiveness, followed by stonewalling, or a total lack of communication. When couples stop communicating, the relationship is not likely to endure.

11. B: The greatest amount of variation between people of the same age is found during early adolescence. The onset of puberty may occur at any time over the span of five years, though it typically occurs earlier in females than in males. The changes brought on by puberty are monumental and can cause rapid changes in personality, physical development, and emotional maturity. Teachers need to be aware of these changes, particularly when working with middle-school children. Family and consumer science teachers may need to act as liaisons between parents and their children, as family relationships can become strained during early adolescence.

12. A: When two children have a dispute and agree to settle it according to their mother's opinion, they are engaging in arbitration. In arbitration, two conflicting parties agree to rely on the advice of a supposedly impartial third party. Sometimes, the parties will also establish guidelines for the way a decision is to be reached. In parenting, it can be difficult to settle a dispute with arbitration, since children are unlikely to honor a decision that goes against their interests. Conciliation is a method of settling disputes in which the conflicting parties are simply asked to meet and converse, with the idea that a resolution will naturally occur as a result of this meeting. In mediation, the conflicting parties decide to enlist the aid of an impartial third party as they attempt to settle their differences. The parties in mediation do not agree to follow the advice of the third party. In negotiation, two parties try to agree on terms that are acceptable to both. Negotiation in family life is a bit like compromise. Finally, restorative justice is a system in which the person who has been wronged gets some kind of compensation from the wrongdoer. When parents force one sibling to apologize to the other, they are essentially using restorative justice.

13. C: In general, the children of working mothers have greater self-esteem. There is no one reason for this phenomenon, although one can speculate that girls might be inspired by the positive example of a successful working mother. The other answer choices are incorrect statements about working mothers. The daughters of working mothers tend to be more independent, and they are likely to have a more egalitarian view of gender relations. When the sons of working mothers are unsupervised, their performance in school tends to decline. It is very important for both parents to have a positive attitude about maternal employment, and it is especially important for husbands to support their wives in ways that can be perceived positively by children.

14. C: Structured family therapists assume that during times of conflict, family members will take sides to consolidate power. Although this process is natural, it can become problematic if the groups last for too long or create a permanent imbalance of power. A structured family therapist surveys problematic family coalitions and destabilizes them. The idea that family life is a series of actions and reactions is an assumption of Milan systemic family therapy. This approach to family therapy emphasizes patterns of behavior that lock family members into their roles, therefore inhibiting their personal growth. Behavioral family therapists assume that bad behavior persists when it is reinforced. These therapists strive to show family members how they may be inadvertently rewarding the very behavior they seek to discourage. Finally, object relations family therapists assume that ill will in a family is often a result of negative projection. In other words, the members of a family may attribute their own negative characteristics to their family members.

15. D: One drawback of inpatient treatment for alcoholism is that it is expensive. In addition, inpatient programs are often not covered by health insurance, so the patient and his or her family may be forced to pay out of pocket. The efficacy of these programs is well

established, however. Some studies estimate that 70% of the participants in inpatient programs stay sober for at least five years. Many of these inpatient programs include the twelve-step process, most famously represented by Alcoholics Anonymous. Patients cannot continue to drink while they are enrolled in an inpatient program, since they are living on the grounds of the treatment facility. Finally, it is true that inpatient programs require the personal commitment of the patient, but this is true of all rehabilitation programs.

16. D: According to Piaget, the ability to imagine the mental lives of others emerges during the preoperational stage. This is the second of the four stages outlined by Piaget and typically occurs between the ages of 2 and 7. The ability to imaginatively construct the mental life of another person is called sympathy. The first stage in the Piaget model is sensorimotor, which lasts from birth until about age 2. During this time, the sense organs become activated, and the child learns about object permanence (that is, objects continue to exist even when they leave the perceptual field). In the third stage, known as concrete operational, the child improves his or her cognition and realizes that objects with different shapes may have the same volume. This stage occurs between the ages of 7 and 12. In the formal operational stage, the capacity for abstract thought is developed. When this stage occurs (and it does not occur for every person), it typically occurs after age 12. Primary socialization is not one of Piaget's stages; it is a person's first experience of living among other people. Typically, a person undergoes primary socialization within his or her family.

17. B: One example of role strain is a new teacher who struggles to maintain authority in the classroom. Role strain is any hardship a person encounters while trying to fulfill the socially accepted requirements of a role. Individuals are almost never a perfect fit for any role they attempt to inhabit, so role strain is inevitable. A public speaker who cultivates his or her expertise is displaying role performance, or the conscious fulfillment of a social role's characteristics. A person whose parents die goes through the role exit process, because he or she no longer is in the role of a son or daughter. A child who imagines what it would be like to be a police officer is demonstrating role taking, in which a person imagines what it would be like to fill a certain social role. Finally, a substitute teacher who waits tables on the weekend exemplifies the idea of the role set, or the different roles that a single person can inhabit at a given point in his or her life.

18. E: An eight year-old with the mental age of a ten year-old has an IQ (intelligence quotient) of 125. IQ is measured by dividing mental age by actual age and then multiplying the quotient. Mental age is defined as the average amount of knowledge held by a person at a given age. Of course, this is a rather arbitrary figure, dependent on the prevailing norms of education. For this reason, IQ is seen as a somewhat unreliable indicator of intellectual development. Many critics feel that it ignores intuitive, spatial, and creative abilities. The average IQ should be 100, since this is the score a person will receive when their mental age is the same as their actual age.

19. D: The student is in the contemplation stage of the transtheoretical model of change. In this stage, a person recognizes the need for a change but is not yet prepared to take action. This is the second of six stages. In the first stage, precontemplation, the person does not yet recognize that he or she has a problem. In the third stage, preparation/commitment, the person determines that a change is necessary and begins to collect information about solutions. The fourth stage is action, when the person begins to change his or her behavior. In the fifth stage, maintenance, the person notes the benefits of the new behavior and

strives to avoid falling back into bad habits. In the sixth and final stage, termination, the person has made the new behavior habitual and is very unlikely to backslide.

20. E: Echolalia is an infant's nonsensical imitation of adult speech. Most children begin exhibiting echolalia at about nine months of age. This is one of the steps in language acquisition. There are six such stages: crying, cooing, babbling, echolalia, holophrastic speech, and telegraphic speech. Over the first few months of life, an infant will develop different cries to express different emotions. After six or eight weeks, the infant will begin to display a vowel-intensive warbling sound, known as cooing. Babies between four and six months old typically begin to make a babbling noise, which over time will come to resemble the baby's native language. Echolalia is the next step, followed by holophrastic speech, in which the baby uses single words to communicate more complex ideas. Finally, between eighteen and twenty-four months, the child will initiate telegraphic speech, combinations of words that make sense together. Deep structuring is not one of the steps of language acquisition. The linguist Noam Chomsky posited that language includes a surface structure (parts of speech, vocabulary, e.g.) and a deep structure (underlying meanings of words).

21. A: The major criticism of Levinson's "seasons" of life model is that it overstates the importance of the mid-life crisis. Levinson outlined four major periods of life: infancy to adolescence; early adulthood; middle adulthood; and late adulthood. The major crisis of life according to Levinson was the realization during middle adulthood that the dreams established in early adulthood are not entirely attainable. This brings on the mid-life crisis. Subsequent psychology has indicated that this crisis does not occur for all people and is often not very severe when it does occur. However, Levinson's model does acknowledge the suffering of life and does address the last years of life, in which a person confronts and reconciles with mortality. Levinson also asserts that life transitions are made consciously and with a great deal of stress. Finally, Levinson emphasizes the role of parents in shaping the early years and thus the foundation of a person's personality development.

22. A: Sudden interest in a new hobby is not a warning sign of teen depression. Teenagers at risk of depression tend to withdraw and will not be likely to take on a new hobby. Instead, depressed teenagers lose interest in activities that previously engaged and pleased them. The other four answer choices are common warning signs of teen depression. Depression is also thought to be hereditary, so teenagers with a family history of the illness should be especially alert to these signs.

23. B: The different treatment given to students who excel in math as opposed to those who excel in English is known as horizontal socialization. Horizontal socialization is a fundamental difference in the treatment of people who inhabit different roles. Doctors and teachers, for instance, are treated differently by society, even though one profession is not necessarily prized more than the other. Vertical socialization, on the other hand, is the different treatment individuals receive when they occupy different class positions. Wealthy people, for example, are socialized differently than poor people. Resocialization is the intentional adjustment of a person's socialization, typically in the hope that the person will become better integrated into society. People who are released from prison, for instance, must be resocialized into society. Anticipatory socialization occurs when a person expects to enter a new role in the future and adjusts his or her behavior accordingly. At the end of summer vacation, for example, students might start to adjust their clothing and hygiene as they look forward to the start of the school year. Desocialization is the relinquishing of a

previously-held role. In a sense, all people are involved in a constant process of desocialization, since they are constantly casting off roles and taking on new ones.

24. D: Thrift is not one of the areas of emotional intelligence. There are five such areas: self-awareness, empathy, personal motivation, altruism, and the ability to love and be loved. These areas were outlined by the psychologist Daniel Goleman, who was one of the first experts to suggest that IQ is an insufficient measure of a person. The development of emotional intelligence is also important. It is possible to improve emotional intelligence by cultivating self-expression and learning to listen to one's conscience.

25. A: The United States actually has a higher rate of teen pregnancy than many other developed countries. However, this rate has decreased over the past twenty years, due to effective instruction and the distribution of birth control. Nevertheless, the rate of teen pregnancy remains too high, especially among Hispanics and African-Americans. Because teen pregnancy has such a damaging effect on success in life, family and consumer science teachers are encouraged to treat this subject in their discussion of family life. The Center for Disease Control offers a number of resources related to teen pregnancy.

26. A: An effective time management plan will encourage students to do the most difficult tasks first. This is considered by time management advisors to be the single most important aspect of successful time management, which is increasingly important in an age of information overload and nonstop distraction. This last point is the reason why answer choice B is incorrect: There is no way to eliminate every possible distraction. Instead, an effective time management plan should try to mitigate the damage of inevitable distractions. It is not necessary for a time management plan to be so comprehensive as to include meals, though some students may find it useful to do so. Making lists is the cornerstone of time management, since lists help students to prioritize their tasks and keep from feeling overwhelmed by the many things they have to do. Finally, because a time management plan will be tailored to the life of the individual, it will be different for each student.

27. C: When a daily routine has been established, it is less necessary to create a list of things to do. Making lists is one of the best ways to organize tasks and to keep from being overwhelmed by responsibilities. However, a daily routine makes certain tasks habitual, which can eventually eliminate the need for the list. For instance, a parent might get up every morning and go through the same steps to get his children ready for school. Since this set of tasks is performed habitually, it does not need to be written down. In addition, the development of a routine helps get the body and mind accustomed to performing certain tasks at certain times. Most people find that a routine makes it less difficult for them to find the motivation to perform unpleasant tasks.

28. D: In the system outlined by Hersey and Blanchard, the leadership style that emphasizes the performance of tasks and ignores the development of positive relationships is called telling. Hersey and Blanchard's model, known as situational leadership, describes four different leadership styles: telling, delegating, selling, and participating. These styles are distinguished by the degree to which they emphasize either task performance or relationship building. The delegating style entails little commitment to either function. A delegating leader passes off authority to his or her subordinates. A selling leader is heavily involved with both task performance and the building of relationships. Such a leader is constantly engaged with his or her subordinates, helping them do their jobs and keeping

them motivated. While a telling leader is very involved in the performance of tasks, he or she is not very interested in building positive relationships with subordinates. Such a leader is likely to micromanage subordinates, often to their annoyance. A participating leader is not involved in tasks but is very invested in his or her relationships with subordinates. Such a leader rarely asserts authority over the other members of the group.

29. D: Most of the time, the best way for a family to decide on a vacation destination is to have a discussion and then have the final decision made by the parents. It is important for parents to give their children a sense of involvement in the process, though the parents should retain the ultimate decision. When parents make decisions without consulting their children, the children are less likely to be willing to participate fully. On the other hand, when children are included in making important decisions, they often are governed by emotion or whim rather than reason. The best decision-making system, then, is a combination of discussion and parental leadership.

30. E: Of the given options, the best way to limit a child's television time is to set a timer and turn the television off when the alarm sounds. This strategy has a number of advantages. It establishes ahead of time the amount of television that can be watched, so the child will not be surprised or feel that the discipline is arbitrary. Setting up a timer also creates an objective method of enforcement with which the child cannot argue or attempt to negotiate. In this, as in many cases, it is helpful to create firm, consistent rules that the child can understand. When boundaries are consistent, the child will quickly learn the futility of arguing and will more easily come to accept the limitations on his or her desire. Scaring the child or using other negative reinforcement is a less desirable solution. Merely suggesting that the child go outside is unlikely to be influential unless it is backed up by other methods.

31. B: Group polarization is a phenomenon in which a group makes more extreme decisions than any member would make independently. Management experts believe that this is due to the desire for conformity and the subsequent reinforcement of whatever solutions are first suggested. Rather than critique another group member and create disharmony, participants will often go along and even amplify the first opinion given. Organizational conflict can actually be a healthy thing, since it indicates that views are being aired openly. Social facilitation is a phenomenon in which the presence of others encourages a person to work harder. Groupthink is similar to group polarization, except that it does not necessarily result in extreme decisions. Groupthink is the suppression of reason in the interest of maintaining group cohesion. Social loafing is a phenomenon in which people do not work as hard in a group, often because they feel their contributions will not be respected.

32. B: Members of a family are more likely to be motivated when their goal is well defined. For instance, if parents decide to save for a new car, their children will be more likely to accept material sacrifices once they know about the underlying goal of these sacrifices. People in general have a hard time accepting changes or commands when there is no communicated rationale. In addition, motivation toward a family goal tends to be higher when members volunteer their participation. A tangible reward that seems fair is another way motivation is increased. Also, the members of a family are better able to stay motivated when they can objectively evaluate their own performance and then use this evaluation to make corrections. Finally, motivation cannot remain high when some members of the family feel that they are working much harder than other members.

33. C: Research has shown that a compressed workweek increases employee satisfaction. The normal work week consists of 5 eight-hour days; a compressed schedule increases the amount of work time for each day but decreases the number of days. Typically, the total amount of time spent at work stays the same. For instance, a common compressed workweek consists of 4 ten-hour days. There is not any demonstrated correlation between a compressed workweek and employee performance. However, employees who have a long commute are generally very enthusiastic about such a plan, since it eliminates one commute to and from the office. This advantage would be irrelevant to employees who work from home.

34. A: The first step towards eliminating wasted time is to keep a log of how time is spent. In the chaotic modern world, almost everyone feels as if he or she is moving in a dozen different directions at once. The natural result is the creeping suspicion that time is being wasted and maximum productivity is not being achieved. Time management experts agree that the first step in eliminating wasted time is to determine where it is being wasted. This is done by keeping an activity log for several days and then studying it to find where time is typically wasted. Once the time wasters have been identified, it will become easier to tighten up the daily schedule.

35. D: A five year-old is probably too young to mop the kitchen floor. Mopping requires a degree of upper-body strength that a child of this age is unlikely to possess. However, a five year-old should be able to complete all of the other tasks listed as answer choices. Moreover, children at this age are often very enthusiastic about helping with household chores, particularly if they are given a chance to work independently. At this age, children are interested in participating in adult activities whenever possible, and parents should take advantage of this interest.

36. A: The proper decision-making process begins by defining the problem to be solved. Too often, students start working on potential solutions before the problem has been fully articulated. This leads to half-measures and ineffective decisions. Only after the problem has been outlined in its entirety should possible solutions be considered. It is a good idea to write down these options. Whenever possible, the emphasis should be on long-term solutions rather than quick fixes. In some cases, it may be determined that there is not enough information to make an informed decision. If this is the case, either information should be collected or, if this is impossible, the decision maker should figure out a strategy for mitigating this problem.

37. D: When making a schedule, children should be encouraged to both include some free time and place the hardest tasks first. However, children should not be encouraged to block out long stretches for completing all homework because this would be too vague. One of the hallmarks of an effective schedule is specificity, so large categories like homework should be broken down into smaller tasks. At the least, the child should divide homework into subjects, and it may even be necessary to subdivide subjects into particular tasks. It is important, however, for a schedule to include some free time because interruptions and distractions are inevitable. If a schedule is too rigid, the student is likely to become discouraged when he or she is unable to meet it. Also, it is a good idea to place the hardest tasks first, since the student will have the highest energy and mental resources then.

38. B: Drop-in child care is useful when the regular childcare provider is unavailable. Drop-in child care is a service offered by some daycares and other child care centers. When

parents have a specific need for childcare, when their normal provider is closed, for instance, they can call the drop-in center and see if there is any room for their child. The parents will need to have registered with the drop-in center ahead of time. This arrangement helps child care facilities operate at maximum capacity and helps parents fill unexpected holes in their child care schedule. Drop-in child care can be expensive, however, and may not be a valid option for children with special needs. Whether a child is in school or not would have little bearing on the utility of drop-in child care.

39. D: One disadvantage of dealing with consumer finance companies is that they often charge high interest rates. Consumer finance companies lend money to private citizens who want to make a purchase. There are few lending restrictions related to the purpose of the loan. Because these loans are considered to be risky, consumer finance companies often charge exorbitant interest rates. In most cases, however, they will accept property as security. The high interest rates and predatory business practices associated with consumer finance companies should dissuade consumers from dealing with them unless absolutely necessary. Before entering into an agreement with a consumer finance company, one should consider whether the planned purchase is absolutely necessary.

40. E: Restaurants are the most common employer of high-school students. This assertion is based on data from the United States Bureau of Labor Statistics. The presence of so many students in food service jobs can be useful to both the family and the consumer science teacher. These students will have direct experience with the cost of food, as well as with the nutritional choices available in a restaurant. It is an excellent idea to allow students to incorporate their work experience into classroom activities.

41. A: Borrowers with a poor credit rating will not be eligible for a bank's prime rate. The prime rate is the lowest rate of interest offered by a commercial bank or other lending institution. It is made available only to borrowers with pristine credit ratings, since these people and businesses are most likely to repay the loan according to the agreed-upon schedule. Savings deposits, demand deposits, and certificates of deposit are all investitures made by the consumer in a bank, and therefore do not depend on credit rating. A savings deposit can be withdrawn at any time, while a certificate of deposit must be kept in the bank for a prescribed length of time. A demand deposit is essentially the same thing as a checking account, because the funds within it can be withdrawn at any time and in any amount. Banks are required to have deposit insurance to guarantee that they will be able to return the funds invested by customers.

42. E: Research suggests that children in daycare are better at articulating their desires. It is believed that this ability develops because the child is dealing with a caregiver who, unlike the child's parent, may not intuit demands. The other answer choices are false statements. Research shows that children in daycare are more likely to be aggressive and disobedient, perhaps because they feel the need to advocate their own interests away from home. Doctors emphasize the importance of establishing the parent-child bond before starting daycare. Children in daycare make friends more easily, perhaps because they get more practice at interacting with others. The value of daycare is closely correlated with the quality of the supervision.

43. B: Presidents Kennedy and Nixon did not include the right to affordability among the consumer rights asserted during the 1960s. Businesses do not have any obligation to sell products at prices within reach of the average consumer. There were five essential

consumer rights promulgated at that time: the right to a safe product; the right to redress; the right to be heard; the right to be informed; and the right to choose. The government enforces laws that require businesses to sell safe products or to clearly warn consumers about products that are not always safe. The right to redress enables consumers to receive a refund or compensation of some kind when a product does them harm. Consumers have a right to speak and be acknowledged by businesses. Consumers also have a right to as much information about products as they desire. Finally, consumers have a right to choose among a variety of products; it is with this in mind that the government enforces laws against monopoly.

44. D: It is generally agreed that a family should spend no more than 25% of its income on housing. Although some lenders are willing to give money to homebuyers who will spend up to 40% of their income on housing, this is considered a risky loan. Such a loan is especially risky when the borrower has other long-term debt besides housing costs. As a consumer, it is wise to create a detailed budget before committing any funds to housing costs.

45. C: Purchasing a DVD is a discretionary expense because it is based on personal desire rather than need. In other words, it is an expense made at the discretion of the consumer. Discretionary expenses are those over which a consumer has the most control. A comprehensive budget must include discretionary expenses as well as fixed and variable expenses. Fixed expenses, such as rent, are the same every month. Variable expenses, including groceries, school supplies, and heating oil, are always present but vary in amount over the course of a year.

46. C: For most people, it makes sense to set up a personal budget on a monthly basis. Expenses such as rent and bills tend to be due on a monthly basis, and a month is long enough that brief fluctuations in food costs will balance out. Of course, a person needs to be sensitive to the fact that some months will be more expensive than others. For instance, if a person lives in a cold climate, he or she is likely to spend more money on heating during the winter months. Those who get paid every week or every two weeks will need to make a simple calculation to determine their monthly earnings.

47. B: If Denise has a credit card with an APR of 4.5% and she maintains an average balance of $2500 throughout the year, the account will accrue $112.50 in interest. APR stands for annual percentage rate; it is the amount of interest charged over the course of twelve months. To calculate the amount of interest accruing on Denise's account, multiply her average balance by the APR (making sure to convert 4.5% into the decimal 0.045). The product of this calculation is the amount of interest accrued on the account over the course of a year.

48. D: It is not a good idea to visit fewer than three daycare providers before selecting one. Each of these visits should be thorough and should include a full tour and an extensive conversation with the care providers. Beforehand, a parent or guardian should make a list of questions for the meeting. For instance, one should get a description of a typical day at the facility, as well as spend some time observing the childcare providers at work. Whenever possible, children should visit the daycare facility before starting to go there regularly. Toilet training is handled differently by different provides, so if this is an issue, parents should inquire about the institutional policy. Children should be allowed to bring a favorite toy, blanket, or stuffed animal to daycare. Parents or guardians, especially those for

whom this is the first daycare experience, should visit at least three daycare facilities before making a decision. Finally, parents or guardians should try to discuss going to daycare with their child in a positive manner as early as possible.

49. E: A debenture bond is secured only by the assets and earnings of the corporation that issues it. This is just one kind of bond sold by corporations to raise money. Consumers should be apprised of the various types of bonds offered so that they can make wise investment decisions. The general difference between bonds is the security offered; that is, the way in which the corporation guarantees repayment. A collateral trust bond uses the stocks and bonds of other companies as collateral. A mortgage bond is secured by a piece of mortgaged property, such as an office building or factory. A sinking-fund bond is a form of debenture bond in which the corporation additionally pledges to pay back the money slowly over a long time. A convertible bond can be traded in for common stock at any time.

50. D: The major benefit of vitamin A is that it helps the body produce healthy hair and skin. Carrots, pumpkins, fish, and eggs are all good sources of vitamin A. Help with forming new cells is a major benefit of folate, or folic acid. There is a great deal of folate in spinach and fortified grains. Vitamin C is one of the primary disease-fighting nutrients. It is obtained most effectively from citrus fruits and broccoli. Concentration and alertness are improved by vitamin B-12. It is most abundant in fish, poultry, and eggs. Calcium is a mineral that helps muscles contract. It is abundant in dairy products and sardines.

51. D: The United States Department of Agriculture recommends two and a half cups of vegetables daily. The other recommended amounts are as follows: grains (six ounces); fruits (two cups); dairy (three cups); protein foods (five and a half ounces).

52. C: The recommended daily values listed on food packaging assume a daily diet of two thousand calories. Adult males are generally advised to eat about this many calories every day. Women and children, however, may require fewer calories, while athletes may require more. When one's recommended caloric intake is considerably lower or higher than two thousand, one must make necessary adjustments to the daily values.

53. B: Food manufacturers now add folic acid to their products because it has been shown to reduce the risk of spinal bifida in infants. Folic acid is a B vitamin that aids in the synthesis of hemoglobin, which is required to transport oxygen throughout the bloodstream. Pregnant women, women who are trying to become pregnant, and elderly people should all ensure that their diet includes foods with folic acid. There are also a number of safe supplements containing folic acid.

54. A: Losing weight quickly decreases the metabolism. Nutritionists and doctors believe that this is a form of self-defense by the body, which senses that food is not as available and therefore tries to limit its use of calories. All of the other answer choices are events that increase metabolism. Weight gain always raises metabolism, in part because there is more muscle or fat to provide with nutrients. Muscle burns more calories than fat, so an increase in muscle mass will correlate with an increase in metabolism. Any exercise tends to increase metabolism.

55. D: An ovo-lacto-vegetarian is a person who eats fruits, vegetables, grains, dairy products, and eggs. These people get most of their proteins from beans, eggs, milk, and cheese. There are several other kinds of vegetarians. A vegan is someone who eats only

plant foods; vegans do not eat any meat or animal product, including honey. Lacto-vegetarians eat fruits, vegetables, grains, and dairy products.

56. A: A person should consume 100 milligrams of major minerals, including sodium and chloride, every day. Of course, sodium and chloride can both be obtained from table salt. Some of the other major minerals are potassium, calcium, phosphorus, and magnesium. Trace minerals, such as iron, zinc, and copper, need only be consumed at a rate of 10 milligrams every day. The precise effect of these minerals on the body has not yet been determined.

57. E: Vitamin C is water-soluble, meaning that it is absorbed into the blood stream and can be forced out of the body through urine and sweat. For example, caffeinated beverages can increase the urine stream and thereby diminish the absorption of water-soluble nutrients like vitamin C. Vitamin B is another water-soluble nutrient. Other vitamins, including A, D, E, and K, are absorbed by the intestinal membrane; these vitamins are said to be fat-soluble. Vitamin D can also be obtained from sunlight.

58. C: An overconsumption of protein can put strain on the kidneys and liver. This is one reason why doctors discourage the use of body-building supplements and protein shakes unless under medical supervision. An excessive consumption of protein can lead to general imbalances in diet, which can undermine fitness in the long run. Protein does contribute to the development of muscle mass, but this is not necessarily a problem. Weight-lifting and vigorous physical activities require complex carbohydrates as well as proteins.

59. D: Palm oil is not an unsaturated fat. On the contrary, it is a saturated fat, meaning that excessive consumption of it can lead to heart disease. Coconut oil, butter, and lard are some of the other saturated fats. The other answer choices are unsaturated fats, which are better for the body. In fact, olive oil and canola oil can reduce the amount of cholesterol in the body.

60. B: A calorie is the amount of energy required to raise the temperature of one gram of water by one degree Celsius. In the United States, every packaged food must contain a listing of the number of calories per serving. Also, whereas in the past it was possible for manufacturers to confuse the consumer by indicating odd serving sizes, the designation of serving size is now regulated by the federal government. All the manufacturers of a particular product are required to use similar serving sizes.

61. D: A person who is 41 to 100% heavier than his or her ideal weight is moderately obese. Health professionals have divided obesity into three degrees: mild, moderate, and severe. A person who is less than 20% heavier than his or her ideal weight is considered merely overweight, but a person who is 20 to 40% heavier is considered mildly obese. People who are more than 100% heavier than their ideal weight are severely obese. Moderately obese people are much more likely to have diabetes or osteoporosis, but do not necessarily suffer from these conditions.

62. E: All three of the statements are true. Bulimia can lead to tooth decay, due to a combination of malnutrition and corrosion by stomach acid. Anorexics often have a distorted self-image, believing themselves to be much heavier than they actually are. Finally, bulimia does not always include purging (induced vomiting or defecation). Bulimics may obsessively exercise or abstain from food in order to lose weight. Both anorexia and

bulimia are extremely dangerous and should be discussed at great length in the nutrition component of a family and consumer science class. These conditions are especially common among middle-school and high-school students.

63. B: Dairy products do not contain significant amounts of iron. The other answer choices, however, are nutrients that are abundant in dairy products. Riboflavin is another nutrient found in great quantities in dairy products. According to the USDA, people should eat two or three servings of dairy every day. A serving is equivalent to eight ounces of milk, a cup of yogurt, or one and a half ounces of cheese. People should be careful about which dairy products they consume, as many contain a great deal of fat.

64. B: Vitamin D is known to help the body absorb the phosphorus and calcium obtained through a person's diet. It is present in small amounts in foods like fish and eggs and is especially present in cod liver oil. Vitamin E is a major antioxidant, meaning that it eliminates cells that can have a deleterious effect on the body. This vitamin is found in good amounts in wheat germ oil, milk, and plant leaves. Vitamin B-3, also known as niacin, helps to reduce levels of cholesterol in the blood. It is found in yeast, dairy products, and wheat germ. Vitamin K promotes blood clotting. It is abundant in spinach, cabbage, and soybeans. Vitamin A contributes to the growth and maintenance of body tissues. It is particularly present in eggs, spinach, and liver.

65. E: Stained clothing should be cleaned within 24 hours; after a day, many stains will have set and will be almost impossible to remove. The other answer choices are false statements about stain removal. It is not a good idea to iron stained objects, as the heat is likely to set the stain. Bar soap should not be used on fresh stains, because it too has the capacity to set stains. Hot water can set stains caused by proteins, like blood, milk, and egg. It is not considered safe to wash clothing with chemical stains alongside regular laundry. Although most washing machines are strong enough to remove toxic chemicals, there is no sense in taking the risk.

66. C: Quilting is the fabrication method of stitching a liner fabric in between two outer fabrics. Because this process essentially creates a three-layered fabric, it is used in outerwear and clothing that is meant for cold weather. Knitting is the use of hooked needles to loop yarn threads together. Fabrics made by knitting tend to be very flexible. In stitch-through, a web of fiber is stitched together by a chain of smaller stitches. This technique is also known as malimo. Tufting is a process in which a woven backing has yarns inserted into it, where they are sealed in place with glue. This process, commonly used in the manufacture of carpets, is occasionally used in apparel as well. Finally, weaving is the creation of a network of three yarns, interconnected at right angles throughout the fabric.

67. A: Wool that has been combed into parallel threads and then spun into a fine yarn is known as worsted. Renowned for its strength, worsted is used in dresses and suits. Cashmere is an especially soft form of wool that is created from the hair of a specific Indian goat. Angora is another high-end wool made from the long hairs of the angora rabbit. Polyester is a synthetic textile, meaning that it is not made from plants or animals. It is often blended with other fibers in the creation of clothing. Spandex is a synthetic textile with amazing flexibility.

68. D: When the fuzzy fibers of a fabric ball up and adhere to the outside of the garment, they are said to be pilling. The degree to which a fabric "pills" is one criteria of durability.

- 87 -

Fuzzing is the emergence of tiny fibers from a yarn, creating the effect of roughness on the outside of the garment. Snagging occurs when fibers catch and are pulled out of the weave. Breathing is the ability of a loosely woven fabric to allow the passage of air. Light fabrics tend to be better at breathing. Creasing is the creation of permanent folds in the fabric. Oftentimes, pants will be worn with an intentional crease along the front and back of the legs.

69. B: When it appears on a clothing label, the word *carded* means that the garment was made from short, thick cotton fibers. The use of carded fibers creates a fabric that is soft and strong. When the garment is made of long, straight cotton fibers, it is said to be combed. A combed fabric is smoother and shinier. A garment that only contains one type of fiber is considered pure. Garments that have been subjected to a permanent or durable press are more resistant to wrinkles. These processes are usually noted on the clothing label. A label may also indicate whether a garment has been inspected and that it was not created in a sweat shop.

70. E: Of the given garments, a pair of wool pants would be the most resistant to wrinkles. Because of the thickness of the fiber and the general looseness of the weave, clothing made of wool tends to be very resistant to wrinkles. This is one reason why wool clothing is so useful for travel; it can be packed in a suitcase and not need to be ironed later. Silk and cotton products are moderately resistant to wrinkles. If packed properly, they can be worn without needing to be ironed. Rayon and linen are notoriously prone to wrinkles. Clothing made of these materials must be washed, dried, and stored properly.

71. A: One common problem with silk clothing is that it is easily damaged by the sun. Silken garments can fade quickly if they are not kept out of direct sunlight. For this reason, silk should be kept in a drawer or dark closet. The other answer choices are false statements. Silk is very resistant to abrasions and wrinkles, and it burns very slowly. Silk is renowned for its smoothness. It is considered one of the least coarse fabrics in the world.

72. B: The FTC does not mandate that clothing labels indicate whether the garment contains mink or rabbit. These fibers are considered to be specialty wools; therefore, they do not need to be identified by anything other than the word "wool" on the label. Fur labels, on the other hand, must declare the animal species and country of origin on the label. All of the other answer choices are pieces of information that must be included on a label. The label must name any fiber that represents more than 5% of the product's weight. The country in which the garment was processed and manufactured must be indicated. Only when clothing is made in the United States and entirely from American materials can it be designated as "Made in the USA."

73. C: It is safe to use bleach on cotton if it is done so occasionally. If bleach is frequently applied to cotton or other cellulosic fibers, the fabric may be damaged. Bleach should not be used on any other fabrics, as it has the ability to cause serious damage. Bleach will often dissolve fabrics made of hair fibers, such as silk, wool, and cashmere. Although bleach can be a valuable tool for fabric cleaning, it must be used sparingly to avoid irreversible damage to fibers.

74. D: Of the given fabrics, black satin would offer the best protection against sunlight. Dark clothing tends to protect the body from ultraviolet radiation better, because they absorb rather than reflect the rays of the sun. Moreover, densely woven fabrics like satin have

fewer holes through which sunlight can flow. Of course, black satin might not be the most comfortable fabric to wear in the sun. Dark clothing gets very hot, and sweating in satin clothing can be unpleasant. Many people prefer to wear cotton clothing, because the looser weave allows for superior ventilation. However, cotton offers little protection against UV rays, so it is important to wear sunscreen under the clothing.

75. E: In interior design, the arrangement of elements in a pattern around some central point is known as radial balance. For instance, a dining room might be arranged such that all of the furniture extends out from a central table. The pattern of the radial elements can be based on size, color, or texture. Symmetrical balance is the arrangement of identical elements around a center point or line. This is the most rigidly balanced form of interior design. Gradation balance is the subtle but regular alteration of specific elements in an interior. For instance, a room might include various shades of the same color. Asymmetrical balance is the arrangement of unlike elements that nevertheless creates a balance when looked at as a whole. Harmonic balance is the agreement of the various design elements in a room. It does not entail any particular physical arrangement.

76. B: In a dumbbell layout pattern, spaces are arranged along a linear path, with major elements at either end. This layout pattern is appropriate for houses or buildings in which there are two main places of activity, and it is a good idea to keep the areas separate. A radial layout consists of a number of paths extending out from a central point. This kind of arrangement is typical of offices and buildings with one central purpose. In a clustered layout, several spaces with similar size, shape, and function are grouped close together and linked along a central space or corridor. A doughnut layout, as exemplified by the Pentagon, consists of a circular corridor with rooms on either side. A centralized layout consists of secondary elements arranged around a central point, or axis. One example of a centralized layout is a plaza, in which the central point may be a statue or fountain.

77. A: The Fibonacci sequence, in which each successive number is the sum of the two previous numbers, begins 0, 1, 1, 2, 3, 5. The Fibonacci sequence is one of the classic proportions used frequently in interior design. It occurs often in nature and has been found to be pleasing to the eye. The quantities of the Fibonacci sequence may be numbers of units or distances.

78. C: Housing experts consider air temperature to be the most important determinant of human comfort. There are a number of factors that influence human comfort, but the primary concern for most people with regard to housing is to be kept warm and dry. In general, a house needs to be between 69 and 80 degrees Fahrenheit in order for its inhabitants to be comfortable. The other answer choices are other factors that affect comfort. Relative humidity is the moisture content of the air relative to the amount of moisture that could be in the air at that temperature without condensing. People tend to be comfortable in houses that maintain a relative humidity from 30 to 65%. Mean radiant temperature is the degree to which a person's temperature changes because of radiation. Depending on the air temperature and ventilation of a room, the people and objects within it will either absorb or give off heat. It is more comfortable to absorb heat than to lose it. Air quality is the amount of pollutants and noxious vapors in the atmosphere. Obviously, air quality correlates to comfort. Ventilation is the degree to which the air in a room circulates freely. The amount of ventilation appropriate for a room will depend on its intended use. Kitchens and bathrooms, for instance, tend to benefit from more ventilation.

79. A: Curtains are fabric hung across the window by a rod and cover either the extreme ends of the window or the entire window. The major difference between curtains and draperies is that curtains are hung from a rod and typically lay closer to the window. A louvered shutter is a hard panel in front of a window. The panel consists of one or more planes that can be opened and closed. A grille is a permanent window covering, usually made of metal. Grilles are generally aimed at reducing the amount of light that flows in through a window. A Roman shade is a translucent, accordion-like panel that is raised or lowered with a cord.

80. D: The gross area of the kitchen is 156 square feet. In interior design, the gross area of a room is its area, as well as the areas of any ancillary spaces. Pantries, closets, and similar spaces are considered ancillary. The area of a room is found by multiplying length by width. Sometimes, the length of a pantry or closet will be referred to as depth. If the shape of a space is irregular (for instance, L-shaped), it is best to divide the room into rectangular spaces, find the areas of these spaces, and then add them together.

81. E: Polyester is the synthetic woodwork finish that creates a durable surface. It is an opaque finish, meaning that it obscures the natural look of the lumber underneath. Lacquer, polyurethane, and varnish are the other three popular opaque woodwork finishes. Polyurethane is quite durable as well, but it can be difficult to repair when it is damaged. Varnish can be either opaque or transparent; it is usually easier to apply than lacquer. Vinyl is a transparent finish that is resistant to degradation by moisture and chemicals.

82. B: It is not a good idea to encourage learning-disabled students to strive for perfection. Of course, perfection is an admirable goal, but students with learning disabilities will likely have struggled at times in school and may become discouraged if they fail to reach an impossible standard. Instead, teachers should give students positive reinforcement whenever they make progress. The other answer choices are sound strategies for working with learning-disabled students. Such students can be overwhelmed by complex tasks, even when they are capable of accomplishing each of the constituent steps. Students with learning disabilities thrive when they are given a specific routine for the school day. Such students often become confused and unruly when they do not know what they are supposed to be doing. Students with attention deficit disorder may benefit from lessons that incorporate motion and tactile learning. Because such students often have a surplus of nervous energy, they are better able to focus when they are physically occupied. Finally, dialogue is a great way to introduce abstract concepts to students with learning disabilities. Often, these students need more opportunity to ask questions and receive clarification of difficult concepts.

83. E: The ability to create a personal budget is one of the cognitive objectives of consumer science. Cognitive objectives emphasize intellectual skills, including analysis, synthesis, and evaluation. The creation of a budget requires a student to assemble all information related to income and expenses and to organize that information in a comprehensible table. The abilities to select drapes and restrain consumer impulses are affective objectives, since they require the student to manage his or her emotions and consult his or her taste. The ability to arrange furniture is arguably an affective and psychomotor objective, since it requires physical activity as well as aesthetic sense. The ability to load a shopping cart is a purely psychomotor objective.

84. A: One common criticism of cooperative education programs is that they isolate students from the rest of the academic community. In a cooperative education program, students actually participate in some of the businesses and organizations they are learning about in consumer education class. These programs provide direct on-the-job training and help students make informed career choices later in life. These programs also increase contact between the business and academic communities, which can be rejuvenating for both sectors. Finally, research suggests that cooperative education programs actually increase student motivation, perhaps because they show students the direct application of what they are learning in school.

85. C: Community service is not a focus on Junior Achievement programs at the high school-level. This is not to say that JA programs are indifferent to business ethics. However, the emphasis of Junior Achievement is to prepare students for success in the business community after their education is complete. To this end, the programs administered by JA focus on economics, personal finance, work preparation, and business and entrepreneurship. Junior Achievement is a non-profit organization that is active in most schools due to the support of corporate and private donations.

86. C: The primary focus of Family, Career, and Community Leaders is the family. Indeed, this is the only in-school student organization that focuses primarily on the family. Since 1945, this organization has worked in all grades to promote the understanding of family roles and responsibilities and to encourage communication between family members and the community at large. Some of the particular points of emphasis for the FCCLA are personal responsibility, community service, and family education.

87. A: A needs assessment for a family and consumer science program should begin with a gap analysis, in which the performance of the class is compared to the performance of students at leading schools. While this may involve a survey of summative assessment results, it should also include a look at the instructional methods, equipment, and community support at the respective schools. This process is similar to the benchmarking performed by business leaders, wherein a business is compared to its most successful competitor. The idea is to bring one's own performance in line with the top performer in one's field. The subsequent needs analysis will define the ways in which the family and consumer science program should improve its approach to leaders in the field.

88. C: A list of community resources is not one of the necessary components of an effective syllabus. A syllabus is essential for organizing the structure and content of a family and consumer science class. Many students do not know what such a course entails, so the syllabus should include a clear mission statement and outline of the course content. The mission statement should state the specific goals of the class. The syllabus should also include clear assessment objectives and an explanation of the grading scale to be used. Experienced teachers know that making the assessment and grading protocols explicit at the beginning of the year can eliminate a great deal of trouble later on.

89. A: Dyssemia is a learning disability that might prevent a student from succeeding in a role-play activity. Dyssemia is a disorder which makes it hard to distinguish social cues and signals. A student with this problem would have a difficult time interpreting the gestures and underlying emotions of his or her fellow participants. Dyssemic students require special instruction about reading another person's body language and vocal tone. Apraxia is a learning disability that inhibits the ability to coordinate movements to accomplish a

particular goal. Dysgraphia is associated with difficulty in writing and spelling. Dyslexia is a broad category of language-related learning disabilities that extend beyond reading. Visual perception disorders make it hard for students to identify written words and symbols.

90. E: Of the given factors, an affiliation with the United States government is the least important consideration in the evaluation of Internet research. There are a number of federal government websites that can be valuable for a family and consumer science teacher, but this affiliation is not a guarantee of utility. The Internet can be a great resource for information about family and consumer science, but an educator must ensure that the information obtained online is accurate and from a reputable source. The other four answer choices are factors that should receive consideration when a person is deciding whether a website is credible. Trustworthy websites, especially those connected with universities and government departments, have an editorial board that approves content. The organization that maintains the website should be easy to discover and investigate. A good website is likely to have links to other, similar websites. Just as we can tell a lot about people by their friends, so we can tell a lot about a site by its links. A trustworthy website will be updated frequently.

91. E: A number of high-school students believe that the most important content area in family and consumer science is food and nutrition. Moreover, this is the most popular family and consumer science subject among high-school students. Perhaps this is because food and nutrition are more relevant to the current lives of high-school students, especially those who are concerned with their physical appearance and health. Housing, family development, and personal finance may not yet be pertinent subjects in the lives of young people. It is incumbent upon the family and consumer sciences teacher, then, to emphasize the importance of these subjects.

92. A: The original purpose of family and consumer science education was to redress social problems such as child labor and the repression of women. In the last years of the nineteenth century, Ellen Swallow Richards convened a group of social reform-minded educators at Lake Placid, New York, to develop programs for domestic economy and household management. These programs were the beginning of what has become family and consumer science education. It is important for teachers to acknowledge that the roots of this subject are in social reform. Even now, the underlying intention of family and consumer science education should be to empower students in their family lives by teaching them to manage their finances and consumer decisions.

93. D: Setting up a mock storefront for a retail business is one way to develop the psychomotor skills of elementary-school students. Psychomotor skills are best acquired through physical action. Setting up a storefront is one such activity, since the best way to learn about product placement is to practice it rather than read or be told about it. Learning to calculate compound interest and looking up banking terms in the dictionary are activities that develop cognitive skills. Drawing a picture of one's ideal house is a good way to develop affective skills. The creation of a budget for a school wardrobe requires a combination of cognitive and affective skills, insofar as the students will need to decide which clothes they want to buy and then work out a comprehensive pricing list.

94. B: One advantage of large classes is that they tend to have greater access to resources. Large classes have more students, and therefore more connections to the community. These connections can be extremely useful in a family and consumer science class. Also, schools

are likely to apportion more equipment and financial resources to larger classes. For these reasons, teachers of large classes often have excellent resources at their disposal. The other answer choices are false statements. Large classes tend to create poorer relations between students and teacher, as there are simply too many students for the teacher to establish close relations with each one. Large classes tend to limit the teaching methods that can be used, since some activities are not manageable with a large group. Teachers must keep records for every student, so it stands to reason that larger classes will create more paperwork. Finally, most teachers are more comfortable in an intimate setting with just a few students.

95. A: Experience is not considered a relevant factor when making changes in the family and consumer sciences curriculum. Teachers of all levels of experience should be able to adapt their method and content when called upon to do so. In recent years, there has been pressure for the family and consumer science curriculum to be more closely aligned with general content standards. Teachers do report that knowledge, time, skill, and expense can be significant barriers to change in the curriculum. In particular, many teachers claim that they do not have enough time to implement major changes. The knowledge and skill obstacles may not be the fault of the teacher; for instance, a teacher might not get approval for changes from an administrator who is ignorant about the subject.

96. E: When dividing students up into groups for a project, the best way to avoid gender discrimination is to assign leadership positions to boys and girls in each group. Answer choice D is also a good idea, but it is implicit in answer choice E. Groups should never be segregated by gender unless there is a specific reason for doing so. Also, students should be discouraged from always performing the tasks stereotypically associated with their gender. For example, boys should be encouraged to assume roles related to the arts, while girls should be given opportunities to work with math and science. For most teachers, the best defense against gender discrimination is awareness and a commitment to equal treatment for all students.

97. C: The primary determinant of whether a teacher will adopt instructional technology is perceived usefulness. The cost of the technology is basically irrelevant to the teacher, since it is the school or district that will bear the cost. Student interest is of some importance, since the technology will not be successful unless it is engaging to the students. However, there are plenty of engaging technologies that have little application in the classroom. Geographic location has very little bearing on adoption of technology, since most equipment is available in all parts of the country. Finally, the teacher's aptitude is slightly less important than perceived usefulness, since most teachers assume that they can learn how to use new technologies in a fairly short time.

98. B: The Carl D. Perkins Improvement Act of 2006 mandated that the curriculum of family and consumer science be aligned with general content standards. This act is an offshoot of the No Child Left Behind Act. Its intention is to boost proficiency by ensuring that the content of family and consumer science classes reinforces general academic knowledge. It is part of a general effort to standardize career and technical (formerly known as vocational) education.

99. D: An activity that requires students to describe their ideal home falls within the affective domain. This domain of education encompasses all of the emotional responses to subjects. A child's emotional responses evolve in a manner similar to their intellectual and

physical responses. When students are asked to describe his or her ideal house, they are essentially organizing imaginative elements into a coherent response. This management of the imagination is an important skill. The affective domain is one of three outlined in Bloom's taxonomy. The other two are the psychomotor and cognitive domains, concerned with physical and intellectual skills, respectively.

100. E: Between the ages of six and eight, children should develop the ability to count coins. In the first few years of school, children should learn the values of the various coins, and should be able to assemble different combinations of coins to produce the same value. At this age, children should understand the general purpose of a bank and a savings account. Some children at this age will be able to manage a small allowance. All of the other answer choices are more advanced skills. Making change, comparing prices, maintaining records, and using banking terms are skills not typically developed until at least age nine.

Secret Key #1 - Time is Your Greatest Enemy

Pace Yourself

Wear a watch. At the beginning of the test, check the time (or start a chronometer on your watch to count the minutes), and check the time after every few questions to make sure you are "on schedule."

If you are forced to speed up, do it efficiently. Usually one or more answer choices can be eliminated without too much difficulty. Above all, don't panic. Don't speed up and just begin guessing at random choices. By pacing yourself, and continually monitoring your progress against your watch, you will always know exactly how far ahead or behind you are with your available time. If you find that you are one minute behind on the test, don't skip one question without spending any time on it, just to catch back up. Take 15 fewer seconds on the next four questions, and after four questions you'll have caught back up. Once you catch back up, you can continue working each problem at your normal pace.

Furthermore, don't dwell on the problems that you were rushed on. If a problem was taking up too much time and you made a hurried guess, it must be difficult. The difficult questions are the ones you are most likely to miss anyway, so it isn't a big loss. It is better to end with more time than you need than to run out of time.

Lastly, sometimes it is beneficial to slow down if you are constantly getting ahead of time. You are always more likely to catch a careless mistake by working more slowly than quickly, and among very high-scoring test takers (those who are likely to have lots of time left over), careless errors affect the score more than mastery of material.

Secret Key #2 - Guessing is not Guesswork

You probably know that guessing is a good idea. Unlike other standardized tests, there is no penalty for getting a wrong answer. Even if you have no idea about a question, you still have a 20-25% chance of getting it right.

Most test takers do not understand the impact that proper guessing can have on their score. Unless you score extremely high, guessing will significantly contribute to your final score.

Monkeys Take the Test

What most test takers don't realize is that to insure that 20-25% chance, you have to guess randomly. If you put 20 monkeys in a room to take this test, assuming they answered once per question and behaved themselves, on average they would get 20-25% of the questions correct. Put 20 test takers in the room, and the average will be much lower among guessed questions. Why?
    1. The test writers intentionally write deceptive answer choices that "look" right. A test

taker has no idea about a question, so he picks the "best looking" answer, which is often wrong. The monkey has no idea what looks good and what doesn't, so it will consistently be right about 20-25% of the time.

2. Test takers will eliminate answer choices from the guessing pool based on a hunch or intuition. Simple but correct answers often get excluded, leaving a 0% chance of being correct. The monkey has no clue, and often gets lucky with the best choice.

This is why the process of elimination endorsed by most test courses is flawed and detrimental to your performance. Test takers don't guess; they make an ignorant stab in the dark that is usually worse than random.

$5 Challenge

Let me introduce one of the most valuable ideas of this course—the $5 challenge:
- *You only mark your "best guess" if you are willing to bet $5 on it.*
- *You only eliminate choices from guessing if you are willing to bet $5 on it.*

Why $5? Five dollars is an amount of money that is small yet not insignificant, and can really add up fast (20 questions could cost you $100). Likewise, each answer choice on one question of the test will have a small impact on your overall score, but it can really add up to a lot of points in the end.

The process of elimination IS valuable. The following shows your chance of guessing it right:

If you eliminate wrong answer choices until only this many remain:	Chance of getting it correct:
1	100%
2	50%
3	33%

However, if you accidentally eliminate the right answer or go on a hunch for an incorrect answer, your chances drop dramatically—to 0%. By guessing among all the answer choices, you are GUARANTEED to have a shot at the right answer.

That's why the $5 test is so valuable. If you give up the advantage and safety of a pure guess, it had better be worth the risk.

What we still haven't covered is how to be sure that whatever guess you make is truly random. Here's the easiest way:
- *Always pick the first answer choice among those remaining.*

Such a technique means that you have decided, **before you see a single test question**, exactly how you are going to guess, and since the order of choices tells you nothing about which one is correct, this guessing technique is perfectly random.

This section is not meant to scare you away from making educated guesses or eliminating choices; you just need to define when a choice is worth eliminating. The $5 test, along with a pre-defined random guessing strategy, is the best way to make sure you reap all of the benefits of guessing.

Secret Key #3 - Practice Smarter, Not Harder

Many test takers delay the test preparation process because they dread the awful amounts of practice time they think necessary to succeed on the test. We have refined an effective method that will take you only a fraction of the time.

There are a number of "obstacles" in the path to success. Among these are answering questions, finishing in time, and mastering test-taking strategies. All must be executed on the day of the test at peak performance, or your score will suffer. The test is a mental marathon that has a large impact on your future.

Just like a marathon runner, it is important to work your way up to the full challenge. So first you just worry about questions, and then time, and finally strategy:

Success Strategy

1. Find a good source for practice tests.
2. If you are willing to make a larger time investment, consider using more than one study guide. Often the different approaches of multiple authors will help you "get" difficult concepts.
3. Take a practice test with no time constraints, with all study helps, "open book." Take your time with questions and focus on applying strategies.
4. Take a practice test with time constraints, with all guides, "open book."
5. Take a final practice test without open material and with time limits.

If you have time to take more practice tests, just repeat step 5. By gradually exposing yourself to the full rigors of the test environment, you will condition your mind to the stress of test day and maximize your success.

Secret Key #4 - Prepare, Don't Procrastinate

Let me state an obvious fact: if you take the test three times, you will probably get three different scores. This is due to the way you feel on test day, the level of preparedness you have, and the version of the test you see. Despite the test writers' claims to the contrary, some versions of the test WILL be easier for you than others.

Since your future depends so much on your score, you should maximize your chances of success. In order to maximize the likelihood of success, you've got to prepare in advance. This means taking practice tests and spending time learning the information and test taking strategies you will need to succeed.

Never go take the actual test as a "practice" test, expecting that you can just take it again if you need to. Take all the practice tests you can on your own, but when you go to take the official test, be prepared, be focused, and do your best the first time!

Secret Key #5 - Test Yourself

Everyone knows that time is money. There is no need to spend too much of your time or too little of your time preparing for the test. You should only spend as much of your precious time preparing as is necessary for you to get the score you need.

Once you have taken a practice test under real conditions of time constraints, then you will know if you are ready for the test or not.

If you have scored extremely high the first time that you take the practice test, then there is not much point in spending countless hours studying. You are already there.

Benchmark your abilities by retaking practice tests and seeing how much you have improved. Once you consistently score high enough to guarantee success, then you are ready.

If you have scored well below where you need, then knuckle down and begin studying in earnest. Check your improvement regularly through the use of practice tests under real conditions. Above all, don't worry, panic, or give up. The key is perseverance!

Then, when you go to take the test, remain confident and remember how well you did on the practice tests. If you can score high enough on a practice test, then you can do the same on the real thing.

General Strategies

The most important thing you can do is to ignore your fears and jump into the test immediately. Do not be overwhelmed by any strange-sounding terms. You have to jump into the test like jumping into a pool—all at once is the easiest way.

Make Predictions

As you read and understand the question, try to guess what the answer will be. Remember that several of the answer choices are wrong, and once you begin reading them, your mind will immediately become cluttered with answer choices designed to throw you off. Your mind is typically the most focused immediately after you have read the question and digested its contents. If you can, try to predict what the correct answer will be. You may be surprised at what you can predict.

Quickly scan the choices and see if your prediction is in the listed answer choices. If it is, then you can be quite confident that you have the right answer. It still won't hurt to check the other answer choices, but most of the time, you've got it!

Answer the Question

It may seem obvious to only pick answer choices that answer the question, but the test writers can create some excellent answer choices that are wrong. Don't pick an answer just because it sounds right, or you believe it to be true. It MUST answer the question. Once you've made your selection, always go back and check it against the question and make sure that you didn't misread the question and that the answer choice does answer the question posed.

Benchmark

After you read the first answer choice, decide if you think it sounds correct or not. If it doesn't, move on to the next answer choice. If it does, mentally mark that answer choice. This doesn't mean that you've definitely selected it as your answer choice, it just means that it's the best you've seen thus far. Go ahead and read the next choice. If the next choice is worse than the one you've already selected, keep going to the next answer choice. If the next choice is better than the choice you've already selected, mentally mark the new answer choice as your best guess.

The first answer choice that you select becomes your standard. Every other answer choice must be benchmarked against that standard. That choice is correct until proven otherwise by another answer choice beating it out. Once you've decided that no other answer choice seems as good, do one final check to ensure that your answer choice answers the question posed.

Valid Information

Don't discount any of the information provided in the question. Every piece of information may be necessary to determine the correct answer. None of the information in the question is there to throw you off (while the answer choices will certainly have information to throw you off). If two seemingly unrelated topics are discussed, don't ignore either. You can be confident there is a relationship, or it wouldn't be included in the question, and you are probably going to have to determine what is that relationship to find the answer.

Avoid "Fact Traps"

Don't get distracted by a choice that is factually true. Your search is for the answer that answers the question. Stay focused and don't fall for an answer that is true but irrelevant. Always go back to the question and make sure you're choosing an answer that actually answers the question and is not just a true statement. An answer can be factually correct, but it MUST answer the question asked. Additionally, two answers can both be seemingly correct, so be sure to read all of the answer choices, and make sure that you get the one that BEST answers the question.

Milk the Question

Some of the questions may throw you completely off. They might deal with a subject you have not been exposed to, or one that you haven't reviewed in years. While your lack of knowledge about the subject will be a hindrance, the question itself can give you many clues that will help you find the correct answer. Read the question carefully and look for clues. Watch particularly for adjectives and nouns describing difficult terms or words that you don't recognize. Regardless of whether you completely understand a word or not, replacing it with a synonym, either provided or one you more familiar with, may help you to

- 99 -

understand what the questions are asking. Rather than wracking your mind about specific detailed information concerning a difficult term or word, try to use mental substitutes that are easier to understand.

The Trap of Familiarity

Don't just choose a word because you recognize it. On difficult questions, you may not recognize a number of words in the answer choices. The test writers don't put "make-believe" words on the test, so don't think that just because you only recognize all the words in one answer choice that that answer choice must be correct. If you only recognize words in one answer choice, then focus on that one. Is it correct? Try your best to determine if it is correct. If it is, that's great. If not, eliminate it. Each word and answer choice you eliminate increases your chances of getting the question correct, even if you then have to guess among the unfamiliar choices.

Eliminate Answers

Eliminate choices as soon as you realize they are wrong. But be careful! Make sure you consider all of the possible answer choices. Just because one appears right, doesn't mean that the next one won't be even better! The test writers will usually put more than one good answer choice for every question, so read all of them. Don't worry if you are stuck between two that seem right. By getting down to just two remaining possible choices, your odds are now 50/50. Rather than wasting too much time, play the odds. You are guessing, but guessing wisely because you've been able to knock out some of the answer choices that you know are wrong. If you are eliminating choices and realize that the last answer choice you are left with is also obviously wrong, don't panic. Start over and consider each choice again. There may easily be something that you missed the first time and will realize on the second pass.

Tough Questions

If you are stumped on a problem or it appears too hard or too difficult, don't waste time. Move on! Remember though, if you can quickly check for obviously incorrect answer choices, your chances of guessing correctly are greatly improved. Before you completely give up, at least try to knock out a couple of possible answers. Eliminate what you can and then guess at the remaining answer choices before moving on.

Brainstorm

If you get stuck on a difficult question, spend a few seconds quickly brainstorming. Run through the complete list of possible answer choices. Look at each choice and ask yourself, "Could this answer the question satisfactorily?" Go through each answer choice and consider it independently of the others. By systematically going through all possibilities, you may find something that you would otherwise overlook. Remember though that when you get stuck, it's important to try to keep moving.

Read Carefully

Understand the problem. Read the question and answer choices carefully. Don't miss the question because you misread the terms. You have plenty of time to read each question thoroughly and make sure you understand what is being asked. Yet a happy medium must be attained, so don't waste too much time. You must read carefully, but efficiently.

Face Value

When in doubt, use common sense. Always accept the situation in the problem at face value. Don't read too much into it. These problems will not require you to make huge leaps of logic. The test writers aren't trying to throw you off with a cheap trick. If you have to go beyond creativity and make a leap of logic in order to have an answer choice answer the question, then you should look at the other answer choices. Don't overcomplicate the problem by creating theoretical relationships or explanations that will warp time or space. These are normal problems rooted in reality. It's just that the applicable relationship or explanation may not be readily apparent and you have to figure things out. Use your common sense to interpret anything that isn't clear.

Prefixes

If you're having trouble with a word in the question or answer choices, try dissecting it. Take advantage of every clue that the word might include. Prefixes and suffixes can be a huge help. Usually they allow you to determine a basic meaning. Pre- means before, post- means after, pro - is positive, de- is negative. From these prefixes and suffixes, you can get an idea of the general meaning of the word and try to put it into context. Beware though of any traps. Just because con- is the opposite of pro-, doesn't necessarily mean congress is the opposite of progress!

Hedge Phrases

Watch out for critical hedge phrases, led off with words such as "likely," "may," "can," "sometimes," "often," "almost," "mostly," "usually," "generally," "rarely," and "sometimes." Question writers insert these hedge phrases to cover every possibility. Often an answer choice will be wrong simply because it leaves no room for exception. Unless the situation calls for them, avoid answer choices that have definitive words like "exactly," and "always."

Switchback Words

Stay alert for "switchbacks." These are the words and phrases frequently used to alert you to shifts in thought. The most common switchback word is "but." Others include "although," "however," "nevertheless," "on the other hand," "even though," "while," "in spite of," "despite," and "regardless of."

New Information

Correct answer choices will rarely have completely new information included. Answer choices typically are straightforward reflections of the material asked about and will directly relate to the question. If a new piece of information is included in an answer choice that doesn't even seem to relate to the topic being asked about, then that answer choice is likely incorrect. All of the information needed to answer the question is usually provided for you in the question. You should not have to make guesses that are unsupported or choose answer choices that require unknown information that cannot be reasoned from what is given.

Time Management

On technical questions, don't get lost on the technical terms. Don't spend too much time on any one question. If you don't know what a term means, then odds are you aren't going to get much further since you don't have a dictionary. You should be able to immediately recognize whether or not you know a term. If you don't, work with the other clues that you have—the other answer choices and terms provided—but don't waste too much time trying to figure out a difficult term that you don't know.

Contextual Clues

Look for contextual clues. An answer can be right but not the correct answer. The contextual clues will help you find the answer that is most right and is correct. Understand the context in which a phrase or statement is made. This will help you make important distinctions.

Don't Panic

Panicking will not answer any questions for you; therefore, it isn't helpful. When you first see the question, if your mind goes blank, take a deep breath. Force yourself to mechanically go through the steps of solving the problem using the strategies you've learned.

Pace Yourself

Don't get clock fever. It's easy to be overwhelmed when you're looking at a page full of questions, your mind is full of random thoughts and feeling confused, and the clock is ticking down faster than you would like. Calm down and maintain the pace that you have set for yourself. As long as you are on track by monitoring your pace, you are guaranteed to have enough time for yourself. When you get to the last few minutes of the test, it may seem like you won't have enough time left, but if you only have as many questions as you should have left at that point, then you're right on track!

Answer Selection

The best way to pick an answer choice is to eliminate all of those that are wrong, until only one is left and confirm that is the correct answer. Sometimes though, an answer choice may immediately look right. Be careful! Take a second to make sure that the other choices are not equally obvious. Don't make a hasty mistake. There are only two times that you should stop before checking other answers. First is when you are positive that the answer choice you have selected is correct. Second is when time is almost out and you have to make a quick guess!

Check Your Work

Since you will probably not know every term listed and the answer to every question, it is important that you get credit for the ones that you do know. Don't miss any questions through careless mistakes. If at all possible, try to take a second to look back over your answer selection and make sure you've selected the correct answer choice and haven't made a costly careless mistake (such as marking an answer choice that you didn't mean to mark). The time it takes for this quick double check should more than pay for itself in caught mistakes.

Beware of Directly Quoted Answers

Sometimes an answer choice will repeat word for word a portion of the question or reference section. However, beware of such exact duplication. It may be a trap! More than likely, the correct choice will paraphrase or summarize a point, rather than being exactly the same wording.

Slang

Scientific sounding answers are better than slang ones. An answer choice that begins "To compare the outcomes..." is much more likely to be correct than one that begins "Because some people insisted..."

Extreme Statements

Avoid wild answers that throw out highly controversial ideas that are proclaimed as established fact. An answer choice that states the "process should used in certain situations, if..." is much more likely to be correct than one that states the "process should be discontinued completely." The first is a calm rational statement and doesn't even make a definitive, uncompromising stance, using a hedge word "if" to provide wiggle room, whereas the second choice is a radical idea and far more extreme.

Answer Choice Families

When you have two or more answer choices that are direct opposites or parallels, one of them is usually the correct answer. For instance, if one answer choice states "x increases" and another answer choice states "x decreases" or "y increases," then those two or three answer choices are very similar in construction and fall into the same family of answer choices. A family of answer choices consists of two or three answer choices, very similar in construction, but often with directly opposite meanings. Usually the correct answer choice will be in that family of answer choices. The "odd man out" or answer choice that doesn't seem to fit the parallel construction of the other answer choices is more likely to be incorrect.

Special Report: How to Overcome Test Anxiety

The very nature of tests caters to some level of anxiety, nervousness, or tension, just as we feel for any important event that occurs in our lives. A little bit of anxiety or nervousness can be a good thing. It helps us with motivation, and makes achievement just that much sweeter. However, too much anxiety can be a problem, especially if it hinders our ability to function and perform.

"Test anxiety," is the term that refers to the emotional reactions that some test-takers experience when faced with a test or exam. Having a fear of testing and exams is based upon a rational fear, since the test-taker's performance can shape the course of an academic career. Nevertheless, experiencing excessive fear of examinations will only interfere with the test-taker's ability to perform and chance to be successful.

There are a large variety of causes that can contribute to the development and sensation of test anxiety. These include, but are not limited to, lack of preparation and worrying about issues surrounding the test.

Lack of Preparation

Lack of preparation can be identified by the following behaviors or situations:
- Not scheduling enough time to study, and therefore cramming the night before the test or exam
- Managing time poorly, to create the sensation that there is not enough time to do everything
- Failing to organize the text information in advance, so that the study material consists of the entire text and not simply the pertinent information
- Poor overall studying habits

Worrying, on the other hand, can be related to both the test taker, or many other factors around him/her that will be affected by the results of the test. These include worrying about:
- Previous performances on similar exams, or exams in general
- How friends and other students are achieving
- The negative consequences that will result from a poor grade or failure

There are three primary elements to test anxiety. Physical components, which involve the same typical bodily reactions as those to acute anxiety (to be discussed below). Emotional factors have to do with fear or panic. Mental or cognitive issues concerning attention spans and memory abilities.

Physical Signals

There are many different symptoms of test anxiety, and these are not limited to mental and emotional strain. Frequently there are a range of physical signals that will let a test taker know that he/she is suffering from test anxiety. These bodily changes can include the following:

- Perspiring
- Sweaty palms
- Wet, trembling hands
- Nausea
- Dry mouth
- A knot in the stomach
- Headache
- Faintness
- Muscle tension
- Aching shoulders, back and neck
- Rapid heart beat
- Feeling too hot/cold

To recognize the sensation of test anxiety, a test-taker should monitor him/herself for the following sensations:

- The physical distress symptoms as listed above
- Emotional sensitivity, expressing emotional feelings such as the need to cry or laugh too much, or a sensation of anger or helplessness
- A decreased ability to think, causing the test-taker to blank out or have racing thoughts that are hard to organize or control.

Though most students will feel some level of anxiety when faced with a test or exam, the majority can cope with that anxiety and maintain it at a manageable level. However, those who cannot are faced with a very real and very serious condition, which can and should be controlled for the immeasurable benefit of this sufferer.

Naturally, these sensations lead to negative results for the testing experience. The most common effects of test anxiety have to do with nervousness and mental blocking.

Nervousness

Nervousness can appear in several different levels:

- The test-taker's difficulty, or even inability to read and understand the questions on the test
- The difficulty or inability to organize thoughts to a coherent form
- The difficulty or inability to recall key words and concepts relating to the testing questions (especially essays)
- The receipt of poor grades on a test, though the test material was well known by the test taker

Conversely, a person may also experience mental blocking, which involves:
- Blanking out on test questions
- Only remembering the correct answers to the questions when the test has already finished.

Fortunately for test anxiety sufferers, beating these feelings, to a large degree, has to do with proper preparation. When a test taker has a feeling of preparedness, then anxiety will be dramatically lessened.

The first step to resolving anxiety issues is to distinguish which of the two types of anxiety are being suffered. If the anxiety is a direct result of a lack of preparation, this should be considered a normal reaction, and the anxiety level (as opposed to the test results) shouldn't be anything to worry about. However, if, when adequately prepared, the test-taker still panics, blanks out, or seems to overreact, this is not a fully rational reaction. While this can be considered normal too, there are many ways to combat and overcome these effects.

Remember that anxiety cannot be entirely eliminated, however, there are ways to minimize it, to make the anxiety easier to manage. Preparation is one of the best ways to minimize test anxiety. Therefore the following techniques are wise in order to best fight off any anxiety that may want to build.

To begin with, try to avoid cramming before a test, whenever it is possible. By trying to memorize an entire term's worth of information in one day, you'll be shocking your system, and not giving yourself a very good chance to absorb the information. This is an easy path to anxiety, so for those who suffer from test anxiety, cramming should not even be considered an option.

Instead of cramming, work throughout the semester to combine all of the material which is presented throughout the semester, and work on it gradually as the course goes by, making sure to master the main concepts first, leaving minor details for a week or so before the test.

To study for the upcoming exam, be sure to pose questions that may be on the examination, to gauge the ability to answer them by integrating the ideas from your texts, notes and lectures, as well as any supplementary readings.

If it is truly impossible to cover all of the information that was covered in that particular term, concentrate on the most important portions, that can be covered very well. Learn these concepts as best as possible, so that when the test comes, a goal can be made to use these concepts as presentations of your knowledge.

In addition to study habits, changes in attitude are critical to beating a struggle with test anxiety. In fact, an improvement of the perspective over the entire test-taking experience can actually help a test taker to enjoy studying and therefore improve the overall experience. Be certain not to overemphasize the significance of the grade - know that the result of the test is neither a reflection of self worth, nor is it a measure of intelligence; one grade will not predict a person's future success.

To improve an overall testing outlook, the following steps should be tried:
- Keeping in mind that the most reasonable expectation for taking a test is to expect to try to demonstrate as much of what you know as you possibly can.
- Reminding ourselves that a test is only one test; this is not the only one, and there will be others.
- The thought of thinking of oneself in an irrational, all-or-nothing term should be avoided at all costs.
- A reward should be designated for after the test, so there's something to look forward to. Whether it be going to a movie, going out to eat, or simply visiting friends, schedule it in advance, and do it no matter what result is expected on the exam.

Test-takers should also keep in mind that the basics are some of the most important things, even beyond anti-anxiety techniques and studying. Never neglect the basic social, emotional and biological needs, in order to try to absorb information. In order to best achieve, these three factors must be held as just as important as the studying itself.

Study Steps

Remember the following important steps for studying:
- Maintain healthy nutrition and exercise habits. Continue both your recreational activities and social pass times. These both contribute to your physical and emotional well being.
- Be certain to get a good amount of sleep, especially the night before the test, because when you're overtired you are not able to perform to the best of your best ability.
- Keep the studying pace to a moderate level by taking breaks when they are needed, and varying the work whenever possible, to keep the mind fresh instead of getting bored.
- When enough studying has been done that all the material that can be learned has been learned, and the test taker is prepared for the test, stop studying and do something relaxing such as listening to music, watching a movie, or taking a warm bubble bath.

There are also many other techniques to minimize the uneasiness or apprehension that is experienced along with test anxiety before, during, or even after the examination. In fact, there are a great deal of things that can be done to stop anxiety from interfering with lifestyle and performance. Again, remember that anxiety will not be eliminated entirely, and it shouldn't be. Otherwise that "up" feeling for exams would not exist, and most of us depend on that sensation to perform better than usual. However, this anxiety has to be at a level that is manageable.

Of course, as we have just discussed, being prepared for the exam is half the battle right away. Attending all classes, finding out what knowledge will be expected on the exam, and knowing the exam schedules are easy steps to lowering anxiety. Keeping up with work will remove the need to cram, and efficient study habits will eliminate wasted time. Studying should be done in an ideal location for concentration, so that it is simple to become interested in the material and give it complete attention. A method such as

SQ3R (Survey, Question, Read, Recite, Review) is a wonderful key to follow to make sure that the study habits are as effective as possible, especially in the case of learning from a textbook. Flashcards are great techniques for memorization. Learning to take good notes will mean that notes will be full of useful information, so that less sifting will need to be done to seek out what is pertinent for studying. Reviewing notes after class and then again on occasion will keep the information fresh in the mind. From notes that have been taken summary sheets and outlines can be made for simpler reviewing.

A study group can also be a very motivational and helpful place to study, as there will be a sharing of ideas, all of the minds can work together, to make sure that everyone understands, and the studying will be made more interesting because it will be a social occasion.

Basically, though, as long as the test-taker remains organized and self confident, with efficient study habits, less time will need to be spent studying, and higher grades will be achieved.

To become self confident, there are many useful steps. The first of these is "self talk." It has been shown through extensive research, that self-talk for students who suffer from test anxiety, should be well monitored, in order to make sure that it contributes to self confidence as opposed to sinking the student. Frequently the self talk of test-anxious students is negative or self-defeating, thinking that everyone else is smarter and faster, that they always mess up, and that if they don't do well, they'll fail the entire course. It is important to decreasing anxiety that awareness is made of self talk. Try writing any negative self thoughts and then disputing them with a positive statement instead. Begin self-encouragement as though it was a friend speaking. Repeat positive statements to help reprogram the mind to believing in successes instead of failures.

Helpful Techniques

Other extremely helpful techniques include:
- Self-visualization of doing well and reaching goals
- While aiming for an "A" level of understanding, don't try to "overprotect" by setting your expectations lower. This will only convince the mind to stop studying in order to meet the lower expectations.
- Don't make comparisons with the results or habits of other students. These are individual factors, and different things work for different people, causing different results.
- Strive to become an expert in learning what works well, and what can be done in order to improve. Consider collecting this data in a journal.
- Create rewards for after studying instead of doing things before studying that will only turn into avoidance behaviors.
- Make a practice of relaxing - by using methods such as progressive relaxation, self-hypnosis, guided imagery, etc - in order to make relaxation an automatic sensation.
- Work on creating a state of relaxed concentration so that concentrating will take on the focus of the mind, so that none will be wasted on worrying.
- Take good care of the physical self by eating well and getting enough sleep.

- Plan in time for exercise and stick to this plan.

Beyond these techniques, there are other methods to be used before, during and after the test that will help the test-taker perform well in addition to overcoming anxiety.

Before the exam comes the academic preparation. This involves establishing a study schedule and beginning at least one week before the actual date of the test. By doing this, the anxiety of not having enough time to study for the test will be automatically eliminated. Moreover, this will make the studying a much more effective experience, ensuring that the learning will be an easier process. This relieves much undue pressure on the test-taker.

Summary sheets, note cards, and flash cards with the main concepts and examples of these main concepts should be prepared in advance of the actual studying time. A topic should never be eliminated from this process. By omitting a topic because it isn't expected to be on the test is only setting up the test-taker for anxiety should it actually appear on the exam. Utilize the course syllabus for laying out the topics that should be studied. Carefully go over the notes that were made in class, paying special attention to any of the issues that the professor took special care to emphasize while lecturing in class. In the textbooks, use the chapter review, or if possible, the chapter tests, to begin your review.

It may even be possible to ask the instructor what information will be covered on the exam, or what the format of the exam will be (for example, multiple choice, essay, free form, true-false). Additionally, see if it is possible to find out how many questions will be on the test. If a review sheet or sample test has been offered by the professor, make good use of it, above anything else, for the preparation for the test. Another great resource for getting to know the examination is reviewing tests from previous semesters. Use these tests to review, and aim to achieve a 100% score on each of the possible topics. With a few exceptions, the goal that you set for yourself is the highest one that you will reach.

Take all of the questions that were assigned as homework, and rework them to any other possible course material. The more problems reworked, the more skill and confidence will form as a result. When forming the solution to a problem, write out each of the steps. Don't simply do head work. By doing as many steps on paper as possible, much clarification and therefore confidence will be formed. Do this with as many homework problems as possible, before checking the answers. By checking the answer after each problem, a reinforcement will exist, that will not be on the exam. Study situations should be as exam-like as possible, to prime the test-taker's system for the experience. By waiting to check the answers at the end, a psychological advantage will be formed, to decrease the stress factor.

Another fantastic reason for not cramming is the avoidance of confusion in concepts, especially when it comes to mathematics. 8-10 hours of study will become one hundred percent more effective if it is spread out over a week or at least several days, instead of doing it all in one sitting. Recognize that the human brain requires time in order to assimilate new material, so frequent breaks and a span of study time over several days will be much more beneficial.

Additionally, don't study right up until the point of the exam. Studying should stop a minimum of one hour before the exam begins. This allows the brain to rest and put things in their proper order. This will also provide the time to become as relaxed as possible when going into the examination room. The test-taker will also have time to eat well and eat sensibly. Know that the brain needs food as much as the rest of the body. With enough food and enough sleep, as well as a relaxed attitude, the body and the mind are primed for success.

Avoid any anxious classmates who are talking about the exam. These students only spread anxiety, and are not worth sharing the anxious sentimentalities.

Before the test also involves creating a positive attitude, so mental preparation should also be a point of concentration. There are many keys to creating a positive attitude. Should fears become rushing in, make a visualization of taking the exam, doing well, and seeing an A written on the paper. Write out a list of affirmations that will bring a feeling of confidence, such as "I am doing well in my English class," "I studied well and know my material," "I enjoy this class." Even if the affirmations aren't believed at first, it sends a positive message to the subconscious which will result in an alteration of the overall belief system, which is the system that creates reality.

If a sensation of panic begins, work with the fear and imagine the very worst! Work through the entire scenario of not passing the test, failing the entire course, and dropping out of school, followed by not getting a job, and pushing a shopping cart through the dark alley where you'll live. This will place things into perspective! Then, practice deep breathing and create a visualization of the opposite situation - achieving an "A" on the exam, passing the entire course, receiving the degree at a graduation ceremony.

On the day of the test, there are many things to be done to ensure the best results, as well as the most calm outlook. The following stages are suggested in order to maximize test-taking potential:

- Begin the examination day with a moderate breakfast, and avoid any coffee or beverages with caffeine if the test taker is prone to jitters. Even people who are used to managing caffeine can feel jittery or light-headed when it is taken on a test day.
- Attempt to do something that is relaxing before the examination begins. As last minute cramming clouds the mastering of overall concepts, it is better to use this time to create a calming outlook.
- Be certain to arrive at the test location well in advance, in order to provide time to select a location that is away from doors, windows and other distractions, as well as giving enough time to relax before the test begins.
- Keep away from anxiety generating classmates who will upset the sensation of stability and relaxation that is being attempted before the exam.
- Should the waiting period before the exam begins cause anxiety, create a self-distraction by reading a light magazine or something else that is relaxing and simple.

During the exam itself, read the entire exam from beginning to end, and find out how much time should be allotted to each individual problem. Once writing the exam, should more time be taken for a problem, it should be abandoned, in order to begin another problem. If there is time at the end, the unfinished problem can always be returned to and completed.

Read the instructions very carefully - twice - so that unpleasant surprises won't follow during or after the exam has ended.

When writing the exam, pretend that the situation is actually simply the completion of homework within a library, or at home. This will assist in forming a relaxed atmosphere, and will allow the brain extra focus for the complex thinking function.

Begin the exam with all of the questions with which the most confidence is felt. This will build the confidence level regarding the entire exam and will begin a quality momentum. This will also create encouragement for trying the problems where uncertainty resides.

Going with the "gut instinct" is always the way to go when solving a problem. Second guessing should be avoided at all costs. Have confidence in the ability to do well.

For essay questions, create an outline in advance that will keep the mind organized and make certain that all of the points are remembered. For multiple choice, read every answer, even if the correct one has been spotted - a better one may exist.

Continue at a pace that is reasonable and not rushed, in order to be able to work carefully. Provide enough time to go over the answers at the end, to check for small errors that can be corrected.

Should a feeling of panic begin, breathe deeply, and think of the feeling of the body releasing sand through its pores. Visualize a calm, peaceful place, and include all of the sights, sounds and sensations of this image. Continue the deep breathing, and take a few minutes to continue this with closed eyes. When all is well again, return to the test.

If a "blanking" occurs for a certain question, skip it and move on to the next question. There will be time to return to the other question later. Get everything done that can be done, first, to guarantee all the grades that can be compiled, and to build all of the confidence possible. Then return to the weaker questions to build the marks from there.

Remember, one's own reality can be created, so as long as the belief is there, success will follow. And remember: anxiety can happen later, right now, there's an exam to be written!

After the examination is complete, whether there is a feeling for a good grade or a bad grade, don't dwell on the exam, and be certain to follow through on the reward that was promised...and enjoy it! Don't dwell on any mistakes that have been made, as there is nothing that can be done at this point anyway.

Additionally, don't begin to study for the next test right away. Do something relaxing for a while, and let the mind relax and prepare itself to begin absorbing information again.

From the results of the exam - both the grade and the entire experience, be certain to learn from what has gone on. Perfect studying habits and work some more on confidence in order to make the next examination experience even better than the last one.

Learn to avoid places where openings occurred for laziness, procrastination and day dreaming.

Use the time between this exam and the next one to better learn to relax, even learning to relax on cue, so that any anxiety can be controlled during the next exam. Learn how to relax the body. Slouch in your chair if that helps. Tighten and then relax all of the different muscle groups, one group at a time, beginning with the feet and then working all the way up to the neck and face. This will ultimately relax the muscles more than they were to begin with. Learn how to breathe deeply and comfortably, and focus on this breathing going in and out as a relaxing thought. With every exhale, repeat the word "relax."

As common as test anxiety is, it is very possible to overcome it. Make yourself one of the test-takers who overcome this frustrating hindrance.

Additional Bonus Material

Due to our efforts to try to keep this book to a manageable length, we've created a link that will give you access to all of your additional bonus material.

Please visit http://www.mometrix.com/bonus948/westefamconsci to access the information.